LEAVES
OF
MOURNING

SUNY Series, Intersections:
Philosophy and Critical Theory
Rodolphe Gasché, Editor

LEAVES
OF
MOURNING

Hölderlin's Late Work—With an Essay on Keats and Melancholy

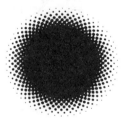

Anselm Haverkamp

Translated by Vernon Chadwick

STATE UNIVERSITY OF NEW YORK PRESS

Cover illustration, "Bäume im Herbst bei Sonnenaufgang," Karl Blechen, 1823. Reproduced with permission of the Staatliche Museen zu Berlin— Preussischer Kulturbesitz Nationalgalerie. Photo by Klaus Göcken, 1992.

Originally published in German as 'Laub voll Trauer: Hölderlins späte Allegorie' © 1991 Wilhelm Fink Verlag, München

Published by
State University of New York Press, Albany

For information, address State University of New York
Press, State University Plaza, Albany, N.Y., 12246

Production by E. Moore
Marketing by Nancy Farrell

Library of Congress Cataloging-in-Publication Data

Haverkamp, Anselm.
    [Laub voll Trauer. English]
    Leaves of mourning : Hölderlin's late work, with an essay on Keats
and melancholy / Anselm Haverkamp: translated by Vernon Chadwick.
        p.   cm.—(SUNY series, Intersections : philosophy and
critical theory)
    Includes bibliographical references and index.
    ISBN 0–7914–2739–0 (hc acid-free).—ISBN 0–7914–2740–4 (pb acid
-free)
    1. Hölderlin. Friedrich. 1770–1843—Symbolism   2. Allegory.
I. Title.   II. Series: Intersections (Albany, N.Y.)
PT2359.H2H34813   1995
831'.6—dc20   95-11833
                                                                 CIP
10 9 8 7 6 5 4 3 2 1

Contents

Mourning Becomes Melancholia: The Leaves of Books

Acknowledgments

Previous work that has gone into the German edition of this book includes:

"Kryptische Subjektivität: Archäologie des Lyrisch-Individuellen." *Individualität*, ed. Manfred Frank, Anselm Haverkamp. *Poetik und Hermeneutik* 13 (1987), 347–383.

"Error in Mourning: A Crux in Hölderlin," trans. Vernon Chadwick. *The Lesson of Paul de Man*, ed. Peter Brooks, Shoshana Felman, J. Hillis Miller. *Yale French Studies* 68 (1985), 238–253.

"Verschwiegener Lorbeer: Im Hofe aber wächset ein Feigenbaum," trans. William D. Jewett. *Hermeneutics and Speculative Philosophy: Hegel and Hölderlin*. Conference, organized by Cyrus Hamlin and Karsten Harries (Yale University, 1987).

"Souvenir de Hölderlin," trans. Jean Greisch. *Paul Ricoeur: Les Métamorphoses de la raison herméneutique*. Colloque Cerisy-las-Salle, ed. Jean Greisch, Richard Kearney. Paris: Édition Cerf, 1991, 263–279.

"Späte Allegorie: Der Name des Vaters und das Bild des ewigen Friedens in Hölderlins Kirchhof." *Bild-Sprache*. Festschrift für Ludo Verbeeck, éd. Luc Lamberechts, Johan Nowé (Leuven: Universitaire Pers, 1990), 81–98.

"Mourning Becomes Melancholia: A Muse Deconstructed," *New Literary History* 21 (1989/90), 693–706. Reprinted with permission of The Johns Hopkins University Press.

The Introduction to the American edition has been written in English, likewise the added chapter on Keats which first appeared, among "Others," in an issue of *New Literary History* on "New Historicisms, New Histories, and Others." Dating from the same time as the book on Hölderlin, the Keats essay marks an impasse of history in any of the many new literary history senses, to which Hölderlin remains alien. Close to a position paper, this essay emerged from the first stage of the project in a graduate seminar in 1984 at Yale on Hölderlin, Keats, and Baudelaire, where it served as a backdrop rather than the foreground from which the analysis of Hölderlin's singular historical position was to develop.

I have to thank many people for the effort to get this little book translated, most of all Vernon Chadwick for his dedication, going back to that seminar mentioned, as well as Cathy Caruth and Bill Jewett, among others. The best I can find now in the book are Chadwick's translations of Hölderlin. As always I'm grateful for Jane Malmo's unfailable help.

Preface to the American Edition

Leer aus geht die Allegorie
—Benjamin[1]

True "mourning" is less deluded
—de Man[2]

This is a book on Hölderlin and allegory, and its title could have been just that: *Hölderlin and Allegory*. Hölderlin research has avoided allegory for several reasons, most prominently because of the precarious distinction between allegory and symbol that dominated criticism after the age of Goethe. The rehabilitation of allegory as a hermeneutical device in the prehistory of Gadamer's "subjectivization of aesthetics" did not exactly fit Hölderlin's sublime failure and, in effect, transgression of such an aesthetics.[3] Adorno's attempt to identify in Hölderlin's style an aim beyond the limits of mere subjectivity and thereby to shift aesthetics beyond the realm of subject philosophy, with Hölderlin as its proto-poet, seemed to move this author even further away from allegory's limited use for the analysis of modern poetry. It was not before Benjamin's exemplary readings of Baudelaire, the other early modern, that the most outdated of schemes—allegory—regained importance, if only of an unclear kind. Still, it seemed, the baroque guise of Baudelaire and Hölderlin's poetry served only the modern subject's mood, and the melancholy of their writing appeared as nothing but a withdrawal symptom, reacting to a lost world order. As a 'discarded image,' to use a very effective term of C. S. Lewis, allegory moved up from what it could no longer represent (but is supposed to have represented before) to the representation of this loss as a project discarded. The oscillation between mourning and melancholia, the deepening of mourning as melancholia, appeared as an aesthetic aftereffect and aesthetics itself as the secularized compensation for the loss to be dealt with. "Aesthetic experience," in this sense, surfaced as the generalized inability to mourn.

Melancholia, however, as Bettine Menke's reading of Benjamin elaborates the point I make with respect to Hölderlin (and with the help of Hölderlin), is the schema not of abandoning but of incorporating the relics of the failed, and abandoned, allegoresis.[4] In Benjamin's Baudelaire, as in Keats, Hölderlin's contemporary, they return fetish-like, aesthetically.[5] Not so in Hölderlin, and this is the point of contrasting him with the English history of melancholy after Burton and Locke or with the other, far lesser known line that surfaces in Racine, Goethe, and Baudelaire.[6] Allegory's end, whether in symbol or in fetish, is symptomatic for what is left behind and keeps haunting but remains, nevertheless, to be read—as what Benjamin has conceived of as "dialectical image."[7]

But Hölderlin, whom Benjamin (as after him Adorno and Paul de Man) recognized as the turning point between the melancholia of the baroque *Trauerspiel* and its dialectic development into nineteenth-century desperation in Kierkegaard and Baudelaire, proves Benjamin's and Adorno's and de Man's intuition in more than the one respect of sublime failure. Empty-handed allegory in Hölderlin remains empty and his late lyric production, after struggling dramatically in the process and exposing its failure in the most concise form, is no longer subject to a ghost dance of abandoned shadows or agony of melancholic rage. There is no Keatsian ending in Hölderlin, but no tragic madness either, as Hölderlin research, no matter how refined its history of madness, believed to have confirmed in his last poems. No merely residual poetic competence as one would expect in states of a growing deterioration, but the candid reduction of a poetics without, or outside of, allegory.

Thus I do not entirely agree with the Lacanian psychoanalyst Michel Turnheim, who was kind enough to approve of my re-reading of Laplanche's Hölderlin and to add further evidence from Lacan's more esoteric writings, but who still understands my rhetorical analysis of the late poems mainly as a diagnosis of rhetorical "abuse."[8] The *abusio*, i.e., catachrestic character of the late poems (*abusio* is the Latin for *catachresis* in the rhetorical lexicon), is an abuse with a future, so to speak. As Turnheim's conception of psychoanalysis as a theory of 'the rest' suggests (of what is left over and 'remains,' even in the Hölderlinian sense of the word), this abuse was to become the very means of an 'apotheosis of the word' in works like *Finnegans Wake*. Turnheim quotes from Beckett's *German Letter* of 1937 (collected in, and as, *Disjecta*) and thus contributes to the notion of Hölderlin the early modern. It is not enough to restrict this modernity to what Hölderlin's reception in the twentieth century could make of his precursorship. Rather, the question is still open, and remains to be formulated, of how Hölderlin's shift from the so-called failure of his late hymns to his seemingly simplistic last (or latest) poems offers an alternative solution to what, with equal right, one could call the romantic predicament of Keats, Kierkegaard, or Baudelaire.

The closest analogue I can think of with respect to a non-Germanistic audience, one which I have already indicated with the name of Cézanne, is the prehistory of nineteenth-century French realism as elucidated by Michael Fried through the notion of absorption in the rhetoric of eighteenth-century religious paintings. According to Fried, the 'supreme fiction' of these paintings is based upon the foreclosure of the observer from the picture (or rather from the depiction) on the premises of a transcendental reference that later was to be reinvested through the 'real.'[9] Hölderlin's dismissal of this transcendental gesture of rhetoric, as in the baroque *Trauerspiel*'s 'overextended transcendence,' exposes the mechanism through which the reinvestment becomes possible. This is not simply the question of a secularized re-usage of the rhetorical techniques involved. On the contrary, the allegory (whose supreme fiction of transcendence seems so miraculously turned into an equally supreme fiction of reference or of the referentially real)

is first to be voided and emptied out, before it can be reinvested; and while the new fiction, beyond its merely fictitious
effects, remains haunted by the withdrawn, the underlying
mediality comes into focus.[10] The late Hölderlin's modernity
rests upon this advanced reflection of 'what remains' (*bleibet*),
and thus provides 'foundation' (*stiftet*), in a poetics of reading
beyond the allegories of meaning, a poetics of the mourning
invested in the material traces of tropes.

Words, Like Flowers:
Hölderlin's Late Work

Hölderlin's late work, so it has been arranged, is defined by the date of his madness. His rediscovery, from Hellingrath's 'rough composition' to Adorno's 'parataxis,' found as a natural border of its theoretical interest the sudden rupture in the poetry as well as the increasing decay of the poet's capacities.[1] Reading the late Hölderlin was thus from the start connected with the reflections of a 'philosophy of life' (*Lebensphilosophie*) and psychiatric speculation.[2] Since Dilthey and Jaspers, such reflections and speculations have regarded the 'other side,' the work of the old, insane poet, as the tragic mirror of mental breakdown in which the highest ambition meets with sublime failure.

The schema of sudden alteration from high claims to the fatality of impoverished circumstances, as romantic its charm and classical its symmetry may be, is for numerous reasons unsatisfactory. It submits 'the work,' the work of his last ambition (until 1804) and his work of 'old' age (after 1806, when he was barely 37), to an overexerted 'logic of production,' as Szondi optimistically might have quoted Adorno, which as 'logic of collapse' (*Logik des Zerfalls*) can justify neither of the two sides.[3] That it concerns the sides of the same medallion, of the same author and his reputation, makes the polishing of the one, shiny side into a one-sided enterprise. The dark, reverse side, pulled from the shadows of madness into the light of serious reflection, betrays the features of an unknown author, unknown, that is, precisely in proportion to the interest taken in the known author.

"Hölderlin's fulfillment," the completion of his late work that Kerényi treated with the aid of the incomplete hymn *Mnemosyne*, suddenly illuminates the darkness that follows.[4] "The other arrow," which Szondi taught us to understand from the lived experience of the poet in the south of France, symbolized "the annihilating power of the divine light" that "drove him, after the trip into the scorching heat of the South, 1802, into benightedness."[5] From this high flight into the light, both of Icarus and Phaeton, follows a plummet into darkness—mythic punishment that demands a sacrifice paid by the reader. His sympathy, that is, his compassion (*Mitleid*) with the poet's suffering, decides everything and nothing; for what can sympathy mean, facing the borderline experience of the 'other,' if not that its impossibility in the difference of madness makes the height of the poet's fall as well as the radiance of his undertaking all the more perceptible. To the *lauriers de la défaite*, which Foucault lets pass in review, belongs the fact that one takes their mythic content literally and takes sickness as punishment for hubris according to mythic standards. The schizophrenia of the poet is thus taken as an instance of anthropological interest.[6]

Meanwhile, punishment follows apace just as "lies have short legs," namely in the manner of proverbs—"as if one had overlooked the shortness of legs."[7] Similarly, in the investigation of "Hölderlin's fulfillment" the other side of his last poems has been "overlooked." As uncontested as the striking break may be between the late work (before 1804) and the later work of benightedness (after 1806), between the poet of *Andenken* and *Mnemosyne* and the poet of *Linien des Lebens* (*Lines of Life*) and the seasons, uncontested also the poet's illness and drastically changed circumstances in life, still the conclusions that have been drawn from Hölderlin's sudden discontinuation of the hymns and withdrawal cannot remain uncontested. The refinement and subtlety of this withdrawal; the hidden reflexivity of the new poetic means; even the 'regression' to already completed texts, as Sattler has shown, a regression, however, with introverted relationships and solutions; hence the very determined negation of already mastered forms—all this suggests other conclusions than simply the limited poetic 'accountability' of the author.[8]

If it is correct, as it irrefutably appears to me in the last chapter of this book concerning two poems from the first, but not yet fully disturbed years of madness, *Das fröhliche Leben* (*The Happy Life*) and *Der Kirchhof* (*The Churchyard*); if it is correct that the question cannot be one of blind refutation, sleepwalking reflexes, or obsessive repetitions—then questions emerge that work retroactively on the reading of what was reflected in the refutation, in the repetition of what has been worked through. Seen in the light of the work of Hölderlin's old age, the shadows of the late work become harsher, and *Andenken* and *Mnemosyne* take on new and different contours. What, as the onset of madness, went wrong with the completion of his life's work—possibly some contingency announcing an even greater consummation—takes on the features of a collapse for which apocalyptic rhetoric is inappropriate. Hölderlin studies have tended to rely on such a rhetoric, namely, to use these symptoms of sickness, the most important of them linguistic symptoms like missing deixis and reduced patterns of interactivity, in order to elevate the intentions of these late works. Contrary to the attempt to make this failure proof of highest intentions, my own tendency here—very provisionally—is to think through anew the achievement of the late and last poems. They are themselves the reworkings of older, in the meantime abandoned schemes and designs. To claim that out of this investigation again comes only a kind of elevation, a surpassing of what was abandoned, would be correct only insofar as undercutting, retraction, and renunciation were not taken as merely regressive moments. Eugen Gottlob Winkler's reading of the whole "late Hölderlin" indicates the direction: "as if here for the first time a destiny were more truly fulfilled."[9]

What is most true for Hölderlin is a holding on to what is to be "kept" in mourning. Beyond Hegel's interiorizing assimilation (*erinnerndes Anverwandeln*), "being true" in Hölderlin is a condition that "seeks and holds the past in its own being."[10] On this demand of 'true mourning' turns the memory of *Mnemosyne*; in it the 'way of *Andenken*' encounters its limit, but not, on the contrary, the progress of Hölderlin's writing (*Dichten*). Beyond this limit his poetry comes to unexpected fruition, which needs no apologies. An artificial blossoming of course, but in the strictest sense the bloom of an appearance in which "Words, like flowers" bear fruit. This development can only be ascertained in the framework of late allegory, which is responsible for the unrecognized continuity within Hölderlin's late work. 'Late allegory' not only in the specific sense that Hölderlin came to it belatedly or that it makes up his late and last work, but rather in the more general sense that his treatment of allegory in its 'truth' (*Treue*) opens a last late horizon of the allegorical age. Benjamin, who instead of a book about Hölderlin wrote a book about mourning, perceived in baroque allegory the first signs of the end of this age of allegory.[11] At the end of late allegory the blooms of poetic tradition bear something other than the customary fruits of reading, 'souvenirs' of lost hope.

Heidegger appropriated the "Words, like flowers" quotation for his own purposes and through his interpretation made it famous. He took the flowers of rhetorical poetics, its metaphors and figures that have given the name to the arrangement of anthologies, as clairvoyantly perceived revelations, epiphanies of poetry, lively living metaphors of the poetic word. No "collection of dried plants," Heidegger objected to Benn's reproachful "herbarium," but rather an "awakening of the widest gaze."[12] What Heidegger makes out of Hölderlin's "Words, like flowers"—and the discussion from Ricoeur to Derrida follows Heidegger in this interpretation, namely a manifesto of poetic revelation through the word—is not so easy to demonstrate when read at the precise place and line of the poem *Brot und Wein* (*Bread and Wine*): *Nun, nun müssen dafür Worte, wie Blumen, entstehn*—"Now for it words like flowers have to originate."[13] The tone of resignation in this line cannot be overlooked. In the *dafür*, which refers back to *nun aber nennt er sein Liebstes*—"but now he names his most beloved" of the previous line, only an ersatz is announced, a substitution through which the word as metaphor enters and enables the naming of the most beloved. The name, which derives from the naming of the most loved and remains as such, is as fresh as it once was as a name, that is, like dried flowers, catachresis.[14] What remains namely, nominally endowed by poets, are 'dead metaphors,' not living ones, as much as one would be tempted to take them as living. That they are most literally what they are—in their literality translucent—shows a different characteristic than that of lively animation. Yet here I anticipate myself.

For what from Heidegger's perspective makes such a lively impression in Ricoeur's '*métaphore vive*' (although it doesn't need it according to Derrida's reading of Heidegger) is only the most successful common denominator for the aporia of the reading of Hölderlin, which makes its appearance in the rupture that separates his late work from the last poems before his retreat. The spare poetry of his old age becomes impassable steppes when considered within the superior claim of a Heideggerian 'Being,' even though this 'Being,' as the gestalt of withdrawal, maintains itself in these poems more in concealment than in revelation: "it retires into its krypt."[15] Whatever one here would like to credit or debit Heidegger and his influence on the reading of late Hölderlin, above all *Andenken* and *Mnemosyne*, it is clear, and in detail only to be made clearer, how much the evaluation of the mad, schizophrenic Hölderlin owes to the hypostatizing of his previous high ambitions. In other words, Hölderlin's poetry after 1806 fully refutes every eschatological implication of the previous poems. More precisely: the allegory that is negated in these poems, the destroyed eschatology within them, is found archivized—the "proceedings of a birdsong"

(*Akten eines Vogelsangs*) that now sounds different and whose unheard-of insight now reads otherwise.[16]

Unlike Keats's *Nightingale*, "immortal bird," this song endures not in the disappointment of its 'fancy.'[17] Hölderlin's late allegory does not succumb to melancholy, the diagnosis for which he gives in *Mnemosyne*. Rather, it "veers," as Benjamin observed in the overextended transcendence of baroque allegory: not into the afterlife, but rather in the *Happy Life* here.[18] The foil of enlightened mourning, which stands out in Haller's *Unfinished Ode on Eternity* and in Kant's commentary on the "true abyss for the human reason," is the indispensable background for that which Hölderlin's allegory undertakes in the end and, in ironic addition to Kant's joke (*Witz*), performs against Hegel's system. The 'overextension of transcendence,' Benjamin's punch line for the baroque 'play of mourning' (*Trauerspiel*), reaches the limit in kryptic subjectivity: subjectivity withdrawn to kryptic inscription.[19] But the old Hölderlin reaches beyond subjectivity and its kryptic overextension. In the empty afterimage of overextended transcendence, objects of temptation and promise gather anew and beyond all exertion: in "leaves of mourning" (*Laub voll Trauer*), "berries, like coral"—the fruit of Cézanne.

What veers in late allegory and leaps into the nothing of emptied features overleaps the allegorical expectation. The empty representation of abandoned frameworks still has the force of withdrawal symptoms. Late Hölderlin, however, is not impressed with them. This is not the concern of his poems. The dimension of reticence, reserve, secrecy (*Verschweigung* in Rilke), of the structural implicature of the emptied forms, this dimension becomes the new space for the old images of relinquished schemes. Instead of backwards melancholy, from which Hölderlin's *Andenken* took leave, his last poems, the poems after all of his last 35 years, anticipate images like those Cézanne brought before the spectator's eye—a very provisional analogy, certainly, whose persuasive power I do not want to lessen by attempting to demonstrate it across the abysses of specialized disciplines.[20] Cézanne's apples are no longer the golden ones of the Hesperides, but the renunciation they forebode is equivalent to a Herculean deed.[21] Extracted from their mythic sources, plucked from the tree of another knowledge, they suggest a this-worldliness that lights up in the translucent materiality of signs, in the abstraction precisely not of forms but of schemes.

Mourning Beyond Melancholia: Kryptic Subjectivity

Archaeology of the Lyrical Individual (Dilthey, Adorno, Freud)

When Adorno spoke in the late fifties about the "crisis of the individual" and of "individual expression" he was drawing on an old commonplace of the lyric, one which, though long out of fashion, would remain of vital interest up to the 'new subjectivity' of the seventies.[1] This commonplace, according to Adorno in his *Aesthetic Theory*, can be historically localized. "The bourgeois art religion of Diltheyan derivation," he writes, "mixes up the imagery of art with its opposite: the psychological storehouse of ideas of the artist."[2] In contrast to this view, he argues that "the subjective moment of the work of art is mediated by its being-for-itself (*Ansichsein*)"; consequently, "the expressive values of the work of art can no longer be immediately those of life." If Dilthey's *Erlebnis und Dichtung* schema had presupposed the experience of a great moment that "finds its expression" in poetry, this had meant an individual expression insofar as the subject of this expression could be, in the emphatic sense, only the individual. Here the individual, not the being-for-itself of the work of art, is "solely" in the position to express itself completely.[3]

Dilthey's paradigm of such poetry, which became the "voice of life" (*Organ des Lebensverständnis*), was Goethe. Even Benjamin claimed that Bergson's concept of modern experience—which, however, he used in the debate against Dilthey—was "of such a kind that the reader must say: solely the poet can be the adequate subject of such an experience."[4] Thus what separates Benjamin's Baudelaire from Dilthey's Goethe are profound changes in the structure of experience itself rather than in the paradigmatic role of the poet for this experience. Already latently meant by Dilthey (even if in a "naiver" form) is Adorno's point that "the subjective moment of the work of art is mediated by its being-for-itself." Admittedly, the "collective substance" (*kollektive Substanz*)—this is what the passage cited from Adorno is about—is for Dilthey nothing but a moment of anthropological self-enlightenment still untouched by any 'dialectic of enlightenment.'[5] The 'lyrical I'—the expression of a subject in the lyric—has not yet been unmasked as the deceptive self-fiction in which this 'I' individualizes itself as lyrical. It does not yet carry the later stigma of the 'phantom uniqueness' of spoiled identity.[6]

The fictive character of the lyrical 'I,' however, relativizes what still goes by the name of 'expression.' In the difference between the writing subject and its lyrically represented I, the relation between *Dichtung und Wahrheit* becomes unfathomable. No longer can only hermeneutical belatedness be responsible for this but rather, in the temporal displacements of this difference, those perversions of the 'regard for representability' that Freud saw effective in dreams. Expression, in this case, would not represent something prior to expression; rather it arrives belatedly and produces in the deferred act something whose representability is not exhausted with respect to anything present but, on the contrary, permits the disclosure (if at all) of something prior to any representational consideration. Adorno thus describes "the turning of objectivity into subjectivity" that occurs in the lyric in such a way that, "entirely through its configurations," the language out of which this subjectivity is produced in the poem linguistically "imprints itself in subjective movements; indeed one could almost think that it was language that *brings them about* (*zeitigte sie überhaupt erst*)."[7]

Expression, the embodiment of *différance* (as "differentiating momentum"),[8] is owing to a peculiar imaginative power of language: the expression of a subject whose emotions occur as effects of linguistic 'configurations.' The performative force of linguistic configuration, which for Adorno as the capacity for 'imprinting in' (*Einbilden-in*) remains related to the representational regard for 'copying from' (*Abbilden-von*), connects the rhetorical moment of the figural with the aesthetic moment of a *'Gestalt'*—as also in Freud the regard for representability regulates the mechanisms of condensation and displacement.[9]

Conjectures on the Work of Mourning (Freud, Benjamin, Derrida)

In the genesis of 'damaged subjectivity,' the individual expression of which is owing to the configurations of language, Benjamin's melancholy deserves special attention. The individuality of such a subject would have to be sought in the damages whose embodiment has become, in a fluctuating history of the concept, that of melancholy. Yet since, in this history, the difference between individuality and subjectivity has not become terminologically manifest, such a task is not as easy as it would appear. We have no trouble, however, recognizing in Benjamin's diagnosis of baroque melancholy "the narcissistic type of object-choice" that underlies the damage of the subject as one that it not so much sustains as experiences in its narcissistic constitution. As Freud himself remarked, the damage comes to "what one calls one's character" and amounts, in its vicissitudes, to one's 'fate.'[10] The psychoanalytical hypothesis of the narcissistic constitution of the subject on the basis of internalized 'objects' finds its baroque point in Benjamin's observation that the melancholy gaze presupposes the death of the observed object, even necessitates it, in order to save it eternally and thereby save itself.

There is a clear 'anthropomorphism' in Freud's concept of narcissism, which has its mythical development in Lacan's 'mirror stage' and its historical paradigm in Benjamin's baroque melancholic. The fact that the object of melancholy contemplation, as Benjamin says in a similar passage, can be nothing but the melancholic himself corresponds to the narcissistic 'regression' in which "the narcissistic identification with the object becomes the replacement of the erotic investment."[11] Actually, the identification here would consist of an introjection that incorporates all objects. Indifferent before the eye of the melancholic, objects remain outside, dead. Thus, according to Benjamin's alternative view, "If the object under the gaze of melancholy becomes allegoric, this gaze lets life flow from it, leaves it behind dead yet secured in eternity; in this manner it lies before the allegorical man, surrendered to his grace and disfavor."[12]

Read alongside Benjamin, Freud has not only the advantage of gaining historical pertinence but also that of the clarification of the concept—here of "character and fate" or "mourning and melancholy." When Benjamin, in reference to the 'play of mourning' (*Trauerspiel*), insists that "the subject of destiny is indeterminable," the hidden polemic is still to be explained in a Freudian direction.[13] In *Character and Fate* this relation remains questionable throughout. Not so in the different 'theory of mourning' that Benjamin announces in his book on baroque tragedy. In the latter case, even if the name is not mentioned, the signs of an encounter with Freud are unmistakable. In the derivation of melancholy from mourning, in the comprehension of its increased, "heavy measure of sadness," hence in the common root of the work of mourning, Benjamin obviously agrees with Freud and speaks of an "incomparably fruitful relationship."[14] As he contemplates it, however, the 'phenomenology' of this relationship undermines the heuristic distinction between "normal" mourning and "pathological" melancholy: "Mourning is the state of mind (*Gesinnung*) in which sentiment (*Gefühl*) revives the masks of the evacuated world in order to take an enigmatic pleasure in its glance." This origin of melancholy that is "mindful" of mourning confirms Freud's insight that in mourning things happen "consciously."[15] The regressive moment of 'resuscitation' contains a conscious feature that must be accounted for by the phenomenology of mourning: "the theory of mourning," Benjamin discovers, "is thus only to be elaborated in the description of the world that surfaces under the gaze of the melancholic." The world that is to be described as the 'a priori object' of mourning has its own intramundane 'objectivity' to which he who wants to 'decipher' melancholy must subscribe. The intersubjectivity of this world, one might add, is one that is fragmented; its melancholy embodies a manner of givenness whose objectivity is produced under the gaze of the melancholic.

According to Benjamin, Freud's work of mourning seems to overestimate the straightforward accomplishment of its business, in the course of which it would first have to be carried out in melancholy and have its exemplary effect in an endless labor, not a final success. Freud himself only apparently opposes this objection when he casually remarks that it is "tempting to seek the way to a description of the work performed in melancholy from conjectures on the work of mourning."[16] Conversely, his conjectures on the work of mourning gain their focus only with the presentation of melancholy. Benjamin, however, in a characteristic *méconnaissance* of sorts, 'mistakes' the work aspect of mourning and sees in the interminability of its effort a lingering—a difference that one could reformulate in terms of a 'rhetoric of temporality.' In contrast to the melancholy of the repetition-compulsion in allegory, the irony of endless initiatives could be interpreted as an antidote.[17] Yet this presupposes a reformulation of the concept of allegory (as one having passed through melancholy) and the clarification of the work of mourning (as it is fulfilled in melancholy).

Writing on the Krypt
(Derrida, Abraham, Torok)

In the center of the work of mourning—which Benjamin sees working contemplatively in melancholy while Freud sees it more actively at work in mourning itelf—there is a problematic 'object-relation' that culminates in an interiorization for Freud, an exteriorization for Benjamin. The projectively resuscitated world is the counterpart of the introjectively evacuated one. The theoretical surplus of the term introjection is taken up by Freud in the concept of identification, which implies an intersubjective momentum. Within the framework of identification the concept of introjection aims beyond mere object-relation towards the "discovery of the subject in the object."[18] The work of mourning is the touchstone of this intersubjective momentum of which the metaphor of incorporation can give no good account. From the outset, Ferenczi and Abraham sought to keep within limits the magical implications of this metaphoric: they define it as 'ego-extension' in contrast to the 'impoverishment' of projection. Introjection "does not retreat, it acquires, propagates itself, assimilates, advances," Ferenczi explains; "if he [man] loves an object, then he takes it into his Self."[19] In this version, the paradigmatic role of oral incorporation is hardly problematic for the later introjective relationship to the world, but evident as it is it doesn't clarify much. Thus in mourning an infantile situation is revived and the importance of incorporation for the introjective capacity becomes obvious.[20] What then follows from the metaphorical potential of incorporation within a life history would be the importance of mourning for the constitution of the subject as a 'system of introjections.'

After early research by Melanie Klein, Maria Torok worked through this consequence and, together with Nicolas Abraham, formulated it into a metapsychological theory, one which Derrida, in turn, has generalized. In Derrida's work it characterizes the point at which the problem of 'individuality' (and not merely the 'singularity' of Limited Inc.) becomes imperative.[21] Under the guiding theme of "Deuil ou Mélancholie" Torok and Abraham achieve a methodical separation of incorporation and introjection that explains how the relapse into incorporation arises when introjection fails. What is no longer accessible as the lost object of introjection becomes fantasmatically incorporated. Already at this point a certain congeniality to the metaphor of reading as incorporation becomes clear, which—from the spiritual food of monks to the spiritual supper of Hegel—delineates the oral libido as the preferential figure of *compensatio* that hovers before the act of reading. In reading, tradition could compensate for what, as *recompensatio*, it is not otherwise capable of redeeming. Hence the significance of the Benjaminian concept of mourning for the philosophy of history. Torok's summary gives the individual variant to this general eschatology of the concept: "The incorporated object, in place and instead of the lost object, will always restore (by its existence and by allusion to its contents) something other than what is lost: the striking desire of repression. A commemorative monument, the incorporated object marks the place, the date, the circumstances in which such-and-such a desire was barred from introjection: so many tombs in the life of the Self."[22]

The system of introjections becomes in melancholy the graveyard of introjects excreted by the process of introjection. The ambivalence-conflict that counteracts the conclusion of the work of mourning discloses with the loss of the object its previously incomplete introjection, which now takes refuge in incorporation. For Freud himself, the ego almost lets itself be corrupted in the work of mourning; "by the sum of narcissistic satisfactions in being alive" it is "persuaded," as Freud has it, "to sever its ties to the abolished object." In the work of melancholy, on the other hand, amid a "host of individual battles for the object . . . the endangered libidinal investment" is finally withdrawn, "but only in order to retreat to the site of the ego from which it had departed."[23] The "fundamental analogy" that Freud offers "between the work of melancholy and that of mourning" is thus made at the expense of the object that, in any case lost, no longer exists and now has to be abolished (*vernichtet*). The analogy is fundamental in that it conceals another conflict between the corruptibility of the ego and the preservation of the object, one which presupposes the discovery of the other in the object to which it aspires beyond its loss. As Derrida has pointed out, incorporation has to do with the conflict of an 'impossible mourning.'[24] "The question could certainly be raised whether this mourning preserves the *other as other* (as dead living) inside me,"is the slashing point of his intervention.[25]

In fact, incorporation, as Torok and Abraham describe it, does not only happen in the place of introjection (of the successful introjection) but stands opposed to introjection in the rejection of the work of mourning and the libidinal reorganization that that rejection demands. It would appear that incorporation enacts in the dead object what it fails to achieve in the living one: it plays introjection in order to stage in this play a preservation whose seriousness is never tested and whose impossibility therefore remains beyond question. It is no longer simply the oral origin of introjection but also its result that accounts for the contradictory nature of incorporation. Unlike in the successful introjection, in incorporation the fantasmatic transition from outside to inside remains problematic and with it the metaphorics of incorporation itself. Derrida is correct in speaking of an 'other topology' and inside of this of an 'other enclosure' (*for*): The walls of the 'krypt,' within which incorporation has its end, "do not simply separate an inner forum (*for intérieur*) from an outer forum (*for extérieur*). They make out of the inner forum an outside excluded in the interior of the inside." As the translators have correctly seen and remarked, Derrida plays with the origination of 'conscience' out of the ecclesiastically guaranteed expectation of salvation (*for intérieur*), with the development of an individual eschatology that is not simply to be conceived of as the interiorization of an external tribunal (*for extérieur*).[26] Elias has described this process as the interiorization of an outside-inside difference; Benjamin saw the allegory of the nineteenth century "colonizing inner life."[27] The hermeneutical problematic of this hypothesis now needs a new formulation.

With the other typology of the 'krypt' (and the new metaphoric of 'graves' associated with it) another hermeneutic than that of the 'fusion of horizons' (with its metaphoric of 'modes of vision') becomes necessary, but also a different archaeology than that of the subject (with its metaphoric of 'excavation').[28] The allegorical model of this hermeneutic is put into question even in its psychologically more refined version. The 'kryptic' interpretation can no longer proceed according to considerations of 'representability' (*Rücksicht auf Darstellbarkeit*) but rather only with regard to concealment as it has been pursued, for example, in the hermetic tradition. Hence the metapsychological tendency of Abraham, Torok, and Derrida.[29] The hermeneutics of experience, one can say, fails vis-à-vis the hermetic of symptoms. Thus Benjamin's phenomenology of the 'melancholic gaze' surveys a hermeneutically uncertain frontier: Allegory as expression of an incurable history is the 'schema' of the melancholy subject who has become absorbed in himself—a schema of melancholy representability.

Just as the melancholic text may be constituted as the text of the melancholiac, so also hermeneutics as the melancholic act of reading. This approach comes to an impasse in the case of the schizophrenic and psychotic text where it may not suffice simply to conclude that they were written by schizophrenics or psychotics.[30] It may explain these texts and make them plausible, but with a credibility now no longer fit for 'understanding.' It lies in the enigmatic shadows of Benjamin's melancholy that the melancholiac sees de-constructed in the allegorical composition of the text at best his own narcissistic constitution: no universal individuality (*individuell Allgemeines*) but a subjective universal (*subjectiv Allgemeines*) in a vanishing world. Benjamin, though, envisages beyond melancholic mourning something incomparably more heroic, a post-melancholy phenomenon that he observed in Baudelaire's 'spleen.' "Allegorical contemplation" neither "veers" into redemption nor does it content itself with a resigned self-enlightenment. What makes it heroic is the endurance of a "continuous deepening of its intention"—thus Benjamin's last word on the subject.[31]

A deepening of this kind, which corresponds to allegorical absorption and opposes melancholy lingering to the work of mourning, is what is meant in the metaphoric of incorporation beyond introjection and in the metaphoric of the krypt beyond archaeology. As "an outside excluded from the interior of the inside," the place of this deepening remains inaccessible from inside as well as from out, "a-topical." What for the baroque melancholiac was left behind outside, dead, is now left behind inside—"living dead." Derrida speaks of a "contract with the dead" ("mortgage") that the krypt thus "perhaps" is—a one-sided contract to the benefit of the survivor. "Speculating on Freud" and his growing involvement in mourning, Derrida quotes from a letter Freud wrote to Felix Deutsch "that the working through of mourning elaborates itself in the depths"; it remains in 'mid-mourning' (*demi-deuil*), as Derrida calls its efficiency rather than heroism.[32] Compare Freud's well-known remark: "the corpse must remain dead, in its place as corpse; one must at all times be assured of this. It must not return, nor be allowed to return and with it the dream of the lost object . . . "[33] As a one-sided contract, the mimicry of introjection, which incorporation performs in the erection of the krypt, contains a communicative momentum of self-staging by which a hermeneutical gaze, though not a melancholic one, is attracted. Derrida elsewhere has cited Levinas's 'trace of the other' whose monument—pathological and poetic—is represented by the krypt of impossible mourning.

The phenomenology of traces or the hermeneutic of symptoms (both self-contradictory like the *a-topos* of the krypt) proceeds from the fact that "their signification" (both the trace's and the symptom's), as Levinas says, is "independent of any intention to give a sign and independent of any project whose intention would be this signification."[34] The point is that it does not need communication, although Benjamin's 'deepening' of mourning and Derrida's quasi-contract of the krypt presuppose a project whose intention surreptitiously wrests from the signification of signs another meaning. The trace therefore "remains specifically a trace," Levinas continues, only when the independence from every signification has become manifest in the termination of every indication: "In the trace an absolutely completed past has passed away." As "something irreversibly past," the lost object becomes the no-longer-introjectable other or, more precisely, the part of the self that can no longer be re-introjected through the other: the corpse is this other's external 'emblem' (Benjamin), the 'exquisite cadaver' its inner secret (Torok). Only in death does the other first prove itself as other; in the krypt it would remain as this other, spared and preserved. The locus of this krypt, however, founds—in its inacessibility rather than in its concealment—that unavailable part of the ego that constitutes itself beyond its introjects, 'objectifies' itself not as subject but as other: "what has been sustained is not a wound of the subject but the loss of an object."[35] What mourning ultimately makes impossible is a decentered self-relationship that is no longer soluble with respect to the other, a relationship in which the self, projected onto the other, returns to the self as other: "*refuse le deuil* and its consequences [namely, loss of one's own] is to refuse to introduce into the self the part of oneself deposited in what is lost [of the self lost in the other]; it is to refuse to know the true sense of the loss that, in the knowing, would make the self become other; in a word, it is to refuse its introjection."

I will break off my reading here in order to locate the lyrical I in a fragmentary field of a problematic only sketched and just as fragmentary. As a melancholy I—hence the standpoint of the discussion from which I take my departure—the lyrical I carries the stigma of a mere fictive uniqueness, of a subjectivity produced in the act of fabrication that obscures the mode of its eccentricity just as necessarily as it exposes it and makes it thematic in the representation. The individual expression that it pretends to be compulsively disguises its allegations. 'Individual experience' reduces to an individual aspect of expression what as expression should be a momentum of the individual: to paraphrase Benjamin, it reduces to the expression of a convention what must remain the convention of an expression.[36] The krypt, as a structure (or strategy) of decentering, helps us at least a small step out of the predicament of such a formulation. The embarrassment of a certain topology, that is, the embarrassment of finding somewhere in the text something 'unconscious,' is reduced to an adverbial 'unconsciously' that qualifies 'expression.'[37] There, not a simple 'unconscious expression' but an enclosure within consciousness unconsciously comes *to* expression, a split in the ego over which the I 'itself' could have lost no word. It has to do, Abraham and Torok emphasize, not with a "simple [sexual] repression," "but with a duality in the fragmented ego. Thus it is as if a part of the ego vis-à-vis the other played the role of the unconscious and said to it: *where I was, there will It come to be.*"[38] Derrida speaks of a "strategic move to protect a place *certainly outside* or a no-place in place"; Abraham and Torok of a "maneuver for the preservation of this no-place."[39] This place is the object of a "true repression" (in contrast to a "simple" one), which pushes the excluded "word-thing," as something no longer capable of being symbolized, "into the unconscious" (my paraphrase of Derrida's paraphrase).

The metapsychological implications and therapeutic consequences of the Wolfman story will not be discussed here. They would not contribute anything further to the matter at hand. What concerns me is the latently communicative (non-) function of this (a-)topic, in which the subject safeguards the unresolved secret of its individuality. Thus what is it that one should name 'individual' in this subject, divided but no further divisible, if not the trace of the other in the self, the trace of the self that has become unreadable in the other? The hermetic of modern poetry and of the subjectivity 'housed' within it (*in ihr verhauste Subjektivität*) would find its enlightenment in the mute communicativity of this individuality, in the traces ranging beyond all metaphorics: beyond the allegorical, it erects in allegory the krypt, leaves behind in the figure a trace. Beyond the line demarcated by melancholy, Hölderlin will land in old age upon another shore. If the assumption is correct that the work of mourning presents the decisive paradigm of deconstruction in which one can read and decipher how individuality beyond subjectivity persists in the subject, then mourning beyond melancholia would become the deconstructive principle of the individual. And if the exemplary place of deconstruction is the literary text, this is because there 'work on myth' (*Arbeit am Mythos*) has become the work of mourning on tradition. It does not submit any longer to any "eschatological melancholy that lies above the whole," in the sense that there would be "nothing more to say."[40] Instead of compensation for loss and the balancing of deficits, this work consists in the individual working through of mourning. "How would it be, if there were still indeed something left to say?"—Blumenberg's last word frees the field for further work.

In relation to a theory of mourning, as Benjamin sketched it in contradistinction to Freud's concept of the work of mourning, Hölderlin's late allegory discloses itself as a departure from melancholy, before its dismissal for Freud became overdue. As Benjamin's reading of Freud indicates, it makes irrelevant the latter's pathological delimitation of a kryptic subjectivity, which was still comprehensible to an Adorno. The *Trauerspiel* book, which Benjamin wrote not about Hölderlin but about the baroque formation of Hölderlin's background, supplies the historical coordination under which Hölderlin's allegory settled its accounts with melancholy for good. Despite Klopstock's well known role as a Hölderlin precursor, the missing connecting link to complete is Haller's melancholy and Kant's critique, which itself derives in part from Haller's deconstruction of allegory. The aporia of *Andenken*, which *Mnemosyne* brings to an end, leads Hölderlin not into the otherworld of madness but rather back into this world (from which a Haller was not the first to have already taken leave). Taken together, Hölderlin's trees in all their 'shadowings'—figtree, laurel, elder in the different ways of their 'reticence' (*Verschweigung*)—presuppose the gloom of Hallerian *silvae*, the extinction of Virgilian tradition. Before its foil steps the figure of Hölderlin in the prehistory of Freud and his deconstructive readers from Benjamin to Derrida and back into the horizon of a *memoria* in which individual *Mnemosyne* is implicated and, in the implicature, relinquished to the inscription of a pictoriality turned inside-out, both exterior and mnemic (*auswendiger Bildlichkeit*).

I. Silva—Impossible Ode
(Haller and Kant)

Unvollkommene Ode über die Ewigkeit

Ihr Wälder! wo kein Licht durch finstre Tannen strahlt/
Und sich in jedem Busch die Nacht des Grabes mahlt:
Ihr holen Felsen dort! wo im Gesträuch verirret
Ein trauriges Geschwärm einsamer Vögel schwirret:
Ihr Bäche! die ihr matt in dürren Angern fließt/
Und den verlohrnen Strom in öde Sümpfe gießt:
    Erstorbenes Gefild' und Grausen-volle Gründe!
    O da ich doch bey euch/des Todes Farben fünde!
O nährt mit kaltem Schaur/und schwarzem Gram mein Leyd!
Seyd mir ein Bild der Ewigkeit!

    Mein Freund ist hin.
    Sein Schatten schwebt mir noch vor dem verwirrten Sinn;
Mich dünkt ich seh sein Bild/und höre seine Worte:
    Ihn aber hält am ernsten Orte
      Der nichts zurücke läßt
    Die Ewigkeit mit starken Armen fest.

Noch heut war er was ich/und sah auf gleicher Bühne/
    Dem Schauspiel dieser Welt/wie ich/beschäftigt zu.

Die Stunde schlägt und in dem gleichen Nu
Ist alles nichts so würklich als es schiene.
   Die dicke Nacht der öden Geister-Welt
Umringt ihn itzt/mit Schrecken-vollen Schatten/
   Und die Begier ist was er noch behält/
Von dem was seine Sinnen hatten.
. . . .

Itzt fühlet schon mein Leib, die Näherung des Nichts,
Des Lebens lange Last erdrückt die müden Glieder;
Die Freude flieht von mir, mit flattendem Gefieder,
Der sorgenfreyen Jugend zu.
Mein Eckel, der sich mehrt, verstellt den Reitz des Lichts,
Und streutet auf die Welt den Hofnungslosen Schatten.
Ich fühle meinen Geist in jeder Zeil' ermatten,
Und keinen Trieb, als nach der Ruh.

Unfinished Ode on Eternity[1]

Ye woods! where no light through gloomy trees breaks/
And in every bush the night of graves paints:
Ye hollow rocks there! where in thickets erred
A mournful flock of solitary birds whirr:
Ye springs! that flow feebly o'er sterile rush
And the forlorn streams in dank swamps gush/
   Witherèd fields and horror-struck grounds!
   Oh had I here/the colors of death found!
Oh feed with cold showers/and black grief my misery!
Be to me a picture of eternity!

   My friend is hence.
   His shadow floats still 'fore my confusèd sense;
Methinks I hear his words/and see his face:
But he is held at the grim place
   Whence nothing returns
   By eternity's mighty arms.

He was what I am today/and saw the same stage
   Given, as I, to all this worldly show

Hours strike and with a sudden blow
Nothing is so real as it seems.
   Dense night of the dreary spirit-world
Encircles him now/with frightful shade
   Desire alone is all that is left
Of what his senses once possessed.

  . . . .

Now my body feels the approach of Nothingness,
The long load of life weighs down my weary limbs;
Joy flees from me with fluttering wings
To the carefree young.
My nausea, ever more, bars the charm of light,
And casts hopeless shadows o'er the world.
I feel my spirit in every line depressed,
And no drive, but towards rest.

Stanzas I–III and XIV (conclusion)

[Chadwick's translation]

Haller's *Unfinished Ode on Eternity* does not make an aesthetic virtue out of the necessity of its incompletion. The subjunctive impossibility of a belated note *captatio benevolentiae* contradicts the notion of any favorable, and already contemporary, readings that would have maintained that the "Unfinished Poem" is not really incomplete but, in its incompletion, only a confirmation of the inexhaustibility of its theme. Thus Haller's own footnote to the poem:

> So that no one were angered by the lines/in which I speak of death as an end of Being/or of hope/I declare/that all these phrases should have objections that I would have answered/if I were able to bring this ode to an end.

To this end Haller was not capable, and so the objections that he anticipated on account of his treating "death as an end of Being or of hope" remain an embarrassment that can find no alleviation in the inexhaustibility of the theme and one which in the late concluding stanza becomes an ever-increasing nausea. What made Haller for Kant the 'most sublime of German poets,' one could suppose, was this self-confessed theodicean failure. In this respect, it could be seen as a variation of Marquardian 'compensation':[2] the failure of didactic poetry ("torso of a *Lehrgedicht* given up"[3]) demands the sublimity of the ode ("breakthrough of the lyrical"[4]) and makes its incompletion a philosophical exemplum of the limits of reason. However, one cannot tie Haller to an ethics of compensation, the 'emergence with impunity' of the aesthetic, as Marquard so subtly phrased it; he exonerates neither himself nor others but rather remains himself culpable. And because this is true in an individual manner, it suggests, as far as Haller is concerned, an interpretation of the so-called "breakthrough of the lyrical" as an incomplete but clear tendency of individualization in the process of subjectivization.[5] I do not want to pursue this point here any further. On the contrary, my intention is to work out Haller's resistance to the common identification of the individual with the subjective in order then to understand the individual moment of his lyric in and by means of this resistance.

The shy, even at times charming, yet deeply depressed anatomist, which the literary *Wunderkind* Haller became in later life, belongs in a mausoleum, as Enzensberger construed it, of the "history of progress."[6] Already the contemporary criticism of melancholy, above all Johann Georg Zimmermann, is fascinated with the whole affair and, moreover, "angered." He grows angry at the "eight grams of opium" taken by Haller in hopes of mastering his melancholy and the abysses it has opened before him. In his biography of Haller Zimmermann had expressed his admiration for how the indefatigable teacher had spent his "Sundays and holidays . . . anatomizing in his tower."[7] In his later work, *On Solitude*, he turns the same Haller into a terrifying example of what he calls religious hyperorthodoxy: "His melancholy feelings opened abysses before his eyes from which he constantly saw hyperorthodox ghosts arise that, with their theology, blew out all the lights of a more enlightened Christianity."[8] The inadvertent point of such admiration turned into criticism is the uneasiness that makes itself felt in those enlightened souls who believed to have overcome, in "a more enlightened Christianity," what they were still shying away from—the glance into the "abyss." The account Zimmermann gives is as apt as his critique is false and unjust. What attracted this enlightenment's denunciation of melancholy was nothing but the shock of enlightenment itself. "The Enlightenment," Blumenberg notes on the subject of the *Zeitekel* with which Haller was infected, "had more success than it had intended."[9] Kant, not the most uncritical intellect regarding the critique of religion and enlightenment, was clear-sighted in his high estimation of Haller (despite the insufferability of the old man). Quoting the *Unfinished Ode on Eternity*, he speaks in the paragraph "On the Impossibility of a Cosmological Proof of the Existence of God" of a "veritable abyss for human reason."[10] Kant, as Marquard summarizes Heidegger's interpretation, "destroys the metaphysics of finitude."[11] This destruction had, as an exemplary instance, its poetic text in Haller's ode.

In this respect, the introduction of nature in the first stanza is an ambiguity hardly to be surpassed. Consequently, it appears almost as if the poem begins anew with the second stanza, which allows the first stanza to be read from the standpoint of the second (and, that is, differently from the first reading). Thus, based on the highly individual circumstance of this new beginning ("My friend is hence . . . "), critics have sought to read the first stanza as an example of a specifically 'modern experience of nature' in which the experience of the early death of a friend becomes the "shattering experience of the fragile mortality and corruption of everything earthly . . . here the swift death of the friend has darkened his [Haller's] gaze, and he contemplates the world in a basic mood of mourning, isolation, and abandonment."[12] Before the melancholy gaze (in the face of the 'collapse of all eschatology,' one would want to add with Benjamin), nature lies simply there, dead, and forms the background for individual grief. Yet, without further regard for the fact that the melancholy constitution of the subject excludes the ability of individual mourning or, conversely,

the fact that the individual working through of the melancholiac disposition cannot be avoided, this view is deceptive. In
the end nausea seems inevitable. The melancholy experience
of nature, one must add in view of Benjamin's later study of
Baudelaire, is the exact opposite of the 'lived experience' that
is said to characterize the romantic attitude towards nature:
Erlebnisse do not take place in the nature of this poem, and the
fact that they do *not* take place becomes inevitable "where *no*
light through gloomy trees breaks," where the "charm of
light" is "barred" by the experiential weariness of nausea. In
the end, in the catastrophe, Haller assumes responsibility for
that which throughout the poem could not be presented as his
own experience.

The difficult differentiation between the lived experience
of nature and the common melancholy to which this experience in the end yields is futile. The ostentatious negations of
the text itself leave no doubt: The "woods! where . . . *no* light
breaks" are no longer, as in Haller's adolescent poetry, "Beloved woods! beloved wreath of bushes . . . " Yet already this
"longing for the fatherland," which gripped the eighteen-year-
old in distant Leyden, Holland, was no immediate "expression
of his feelings" but a reading of Virgil.[13] If not the baroque background (the rejected 'Lohensteinian taste'), one would at least
have to take seriously the classical background of Haller (his
declared models Lucretius, Horace, Virgil) instead of excusing
him for his vestiges of baroque style and unconditionally bring-
ing him to the right side of contemporary literary quarrels between Leipzig and Zürich, which he ignored.[14]

The *silvae* of Virgil are here thus not merely aids to the
expression of a new literary epoch not yet certain of its own
means. Rather, they are the traditional allegorical locus of poetry, specifically of the bucolic genre, as well as the poetic
place of allegorical interpretation—an allegory of allegory.[15] In
Petrarch, they provide the allegorical background of an indi-
vidually understood autobiography that now could leave behind Dante's *selva oscura*, where earthly life was caught in the
darkness of sin (*Inferno* I, 1–3). Accordingly, the *silvae* are related to a metaphorics of sources that Dante uses for his Virgil

and Petrarch for Homer as the source of Virgil. For Haller, both the place of poetry ("Ye woods!") as well as the stream of traditional reception ("Ye springs!") are "witherèd": "Witherèd fields and horror-struck grounds!" In an additional footnote, Haller mentions *Tofwasser*, "which make the damp meadows in which they flow sandy and infertile." Moreover, Haller's editors never tire of repeating his first biographer Zimmermann who stated that the poem was written "near the so-called Glasbrunnen in the *Bremgarten* forest near Bern."[16] Whatever bearing this can have on the history of the composition of the poem, which encompasses several years, such a referentialization does not contradict the allegorical coherence of the stanzas (nor does it prove an actual experience of the scientist) but rather fulfills in a metaphor what it undertakes in an allegory to present: the mortification of allegory in 'dead metaphor.'

The process of reversal from *locus amoenus* to the "witherèd fields," which present themselves to the anatomist, could not be more complete. In the Augustinian tradition of medieval hermeneutics, the woods were a picture of the secrets of scripture that were to be revealed: "*Et revelabit silvas*: that is, then he will unveil to you the darknesses of the divine books and the shadows of mysteries" runs Augustine's interpretation of Psalms 28:9.[17] In Haller's ode, on the contrary, the darkness reveals itself as shadows of a greater darkness: "the approach of Nothingness" in the last stanza. This nature grants no "earthly pleasure in God," as Haller's contemporary Brockes described it in 1729 in his *Irdisches Vergnügen in Gott*. If the literary pleasure-ground (*locus amoenus*) could have once stood for the promise of an otherworldly paradise, then its complete perversion remains just good enough for picturing the unthinkability of an empty transcendence. What for Augustine was, in the cited passage, the shadows of mysteries (*umbracula mysteriorum*) has become for Haller in the end "hopeless shadows" that death casts before it: "You now shall be my picture of eternity!" This picture wrests once more from the shadows the after-image of dead tradition, just as Augustine had drawn, in the opposite direction, the foreshadowing of revelation (*umbra et figura*) from Virgil.

Haller's resistance to this is hidden in a second reference to Virgil, which marks in the allegory of allegory its hidden typological point: individual eschatology here cancels allegory. Addressed *ad Vergilium*, Horace's *consolatio* "On the death of Quintilius" (*Carmina* I, 24) permits a juxtaposition in Haller's ode of the allegorical model of the *silvae* with the loss of a friend. Horace's ode begins with the rhetorical gesture of the impossibility of all comfort and the call to the Muses for the appropriate lamentation. Like Haller's appeal to nature, a second stanza follows that confirms the friend's death, though with an opposite intention to that of Haller. For Horace's poem is an elegy, while Haller himself is the inconsolable one who knows better than to find comfort in the one comforted by Horace—Virgil. The similar imagery in Horace's poem clarifies the dialectical reversal of the image in Haller's poem: *num vanae redeat sanguis imagini*. Late eighteenth-century translators of Horace like Herder, Ramler, and Voss read 'silhouette' or 'shadow image' (*Schattenbild*) in this line, and confirm the emptying imagination that Haller depicts ("His shadow hovers before me still . . . ; Methinks I see his image . . . "). In Horace's poem this silhouette has its own mythic scene in which, with the fall of Orpheus, the poet invokes the failure of poetry in the face of death. "But he is held at the grim place/Whence nothing returns" is a rewriting of this scene. Up to the second stanza one can read Haller's poem as a counterpoint to Horace, one which resists the empty running of allegory, exposing the impertinence of the received patterns. It refuses comfort, their traditional aim. Horace's last word, *nefas*, not only brings out the futility of comfort, as most commentaries would have it, but also addresses the impossibility of mourning: a failure of poetry that Haller and later Hölderlin carry out in their writing.[18]

In Petrarch (and after him Petrarchism), the Virgilian model of the *silvae* had become the paradigm of a poetic function that had left its bucolic tradition behind: Petrarch's woods are a poetic domain through whose disclosure "the concrete meaning of bucolic pictures" is suspended.[19] For Haller, this domain reveals itself as a wasteland whose allegorical disclosure destroys the substrate of traditional images. The poetic function, however, surpasses the structure whose representation it questions in this manner. The destruction of allegory results in the expression of mourning, which shifts the previous allegory of allegory into a state of *melancholia*: the bucolic commonplace of the disappearance of the muses and the devastation of the *locus amoenus* proves itself to be a means of melancholic self-positing that must devolve to sheer nausea in a poem about eternity. "Allegory walks away empty-handed," Benjamin closes his diagnosis of baroque melancholy.[20] What constitutes the individual expression in this emptiness of Haller's poem and only produces nausea as allegorical residue is to be sought neither in the occasion of the text (the death of a friend) nor in the disposition of the author (his melancholy) but rather in the manner in which the loss of representation turns into mourning, the lost representation becomes a cipher for the bemoaned loss.

The individual opportunity, the sudden death of a young man called Christ, whose name here contributes more to the issue than his identity, is of a specially puzzling nature. Haller's contemporaries knew nothing about him and were thus immediately prepared to go beyond the literary occasion of this friend's death to the doctrinal content of the poem that was to be uttered on such an occasion.[21] The effective middle sections (stanzas IV–XIII) strike like a powerful distraction, before the last stanza brings about an abrupt end. In these stanzas one can easily make out the compensatory moment that establishes a threefold sublime—in the social distribution of roles (IV–V), in the mathematical ordering of time, space, and number (VI–X), and in the biological order of phylo- and ontogenesis (XI–XIII)—that takes the place of the loss of the tropological as well as the anagogical meaning of traditional forms and conventional expectations of life. Unlike in Klopstock, however, the cosmic eschatology and its collective forms of compromise do not get transferred to an eschatology of individual consequences.[22] Yet the failure to answer the question of theodicy, which occurs for him more precisely as a failure of theodicy, constitutes Haller's own death angst. It overextends the baroque melancholy of an already "overextended transcendence," as Benjamin describes it.[23] It is grounded in individual mourning in contrast to the melancholy disposition of the age. As individual, this mourning carries—for Haller more than any other—the heroic features of 'sublime' melancholy (*Melencholia illa heroica*, according to one of Benjamin's favorite quotations).[24] What makes it heroic is its resistance and in its resistance its deepening. Mourning produces this continuous deepening effect and, in sublime fashion, becomes melancholy in instances of repetition, about which Haller was well-versed in song. The little-known friend is the last of these instances and the ode about him his last substantial poem.

It is thus necessary to return to the introductory stanza whose strict alexandrines are an obvious baroque quotation, one that breaks off in the caesura of the last lines in order to introduce a more relaxed meter for the madrigal that begins the second stanza. I do not want to pursue here the underestimation of the baroque side of Haller. Had he not, however, relied on it to a special degree, this transition would be meaningless. I mean more precisely, his reading and imitation of Virgil led, in its conventional baroque form, to a peculiar overinvestment of these repeated traits. Already Haller's first reader and closest friend, his medical colleague Werlhof, had noticed incongruities that may be inconsistent in a 'painterly' sense, but as quotations, follow another logic. For example, Werlhof asks whether "a bird that lives in a *flock* (*Geschwärm*) could be called *solitary* (*einsam*)."[25] These birds are solitary even in the flock because the pleasure-ground is no longer a place of social life but of death, which lurks "in every bush." This point is made in Haller's famous elegy, the *Mourning Ode*, written on the death of his beloved Mariane, in imitation of which—after a continuation in another poem *On the Same*—he set to work, belatedly, on the ode on eternity. In the *Mourning Ode* the following stanza appears near the end of the poem:[26]

> Im dicksten Wald, bei finstern Buchen,
> Wo niemand meine Klagen hört,
> Will ich dein holdes Bildnis suchen,
> Wo niemand mein Gedächtnis stört.
> . . . .

In thickest wood, in gloomy beeches,
Where no one hears my complaint,
Your gracious likeness I will search
Where no one disturbs my memories.

That is not only a basic Petrarchan situation but a quotation from Virgil from the second *Eclogue*, where the shepherd Corydon "under thick, shady beeches . . . in solitude calls out his artless complaint to the mountains and woods" (*inter densas umbrosa cacumina fagos*, ll. 3–5). Again one shouldn't mistake this renaturalization—the intensification of darkness from shady beeches to gloomy firs—for a realistic representation of nature. For again what is going on here is the depotentialization of allegory whose bucolic paradigm the passage quotes. Not an arbitrary piece of scenery, but rather the exemplary scene that, as 'primal scene' of the bucolic, had become useful as the paradigm of allegorization, the allegorical potentialization of the bucolic. The intertextual reproofs prove a supposed immediacy of natural experience to be only the 'after-image' of traditional transmissions, quasi-hallucinatory withdrawal symptoms that accompany the deepening of mourning to the point of satiety.

Contradicting his own paradigm choice of Haller as the 'sentimental' poet, Schiller criticized this poem for having insufficient immediacy:

When Haller mourns the death of his wife (one knows the beautiful lyric) and in the following way begins:

Soll ich von deinem Tode singen
O Mariane welch ein Lied!
Wenn Seufzer mit den Worten ringen
Und ein Begriff den andern flieht u.s.f.

Should I sing of your death
Oh Mariane what a song!
When sighs with words compete
And one thought flees from the rest . . .

although we find this description quite true, we feel also that the poet does not communicate to us his actual feelings but rather his thoughts about them. For this reason, he moves us much less because he himself must already be very much chilled in order to become a spectator of his own emotion.[27]

They are not merely "thoughts" that Haller communicates about his feelings so much as texts through which he—working through—works them out. For the first two lines Haller drew upon Canitz' lament for his *Doris*[28]:

> Soll ich meine Doris missen?
> Hat sie mir der Tod entrissen?

> *Will I miss my Doris?*
> *Was she torn from me by Death?*

The basic perspective of this resumption to a previous text is its impossibility: an impossible enterprise to sing a song about Mariane's death like that of Canitz about Doris. Here no rhetorical question is appropriate, for this subject in question is beyond answers, even if the questions seem to be self-evident. Whereas Canitz' text seems to express a refusal to recognize the loss, Haller's text makes this 'truth' transparent as a rhetorical operation, uncovering the impossibility of the question in the repetition of the question. (An impossibility, to be sure, also Canitz is aware of, of course.) The thought that is worked out in this repetition only guarantees a feeling whose immediate expression lies beyond its reach. Haller's as well as Canitz' question ("Will I . . . ?") is both undecided and undecidable.[29] The 'ambivalence-conflict' that Freud sees carried out in the work of mourning finds its resolution in a confession a few stanzas later:

> Ja meine Seele will ich schildern,
> Von Lieb' und Traurigkeit verwirrt,

Wie sie, ergötzt an Trauerbildern,
In Kummerlabyrinthen irrt!

Yes, I want to picture my soul,
From love and sadness dazed,
How it, enthralled by mournful images,
In troubling labyrinths strays.

The erring and whirring of the flock of solitary birds recalls this moment from this only slightly older poem. Freud speaks of a "trait of insistent garrulousness" that characterizes melancholy. It gives rise to "a satisfaction in its own exposure" so that a "shadow of the object" falls across the ego in such a way that the loss of the object becomes transformed into a loss in the ego and hence its cleavage.[30] In this respect, the passage reveals an ambiguity, as the doctor Werlhof may have guessed and the critic Empson has described: "a fundamental division in the writer's mind."[31]

The baroque language-play of Doris poems, which had in Canitz' poetry long become precarious, is no longer an issue: "It is a play of my youth," Haller excuses himself in a late remark about his own *Doris*, which he had dedicated, in "innocent passion," to his first love Mariane:

Komm, Doris, komm zu jenen Buchen,
Laß uns den stillen Grund besuchen,
Wo nichts sich regt als ich und du . . .

Come, Doris, come to those beeches,
Let us visit the tranquil ground
Where nothing stirs but I and you . . .

Those beech trees of Virgil with which the twenty-two-year-old courted his "Doris" stand the test even in death and enter the lament just at its climax—"what a song!" These trees are the same ones to which, in the deepening of his mourning, the aging Haller had occasion to return. "Haller's Doris," which Klopstock replays and reperforms on the occa-

sion of his *Ode on a Trip on the Lake of Zürich,* is the true pretext of his work of mourning.[32] The loss, around which the
"solitary birds" confusingly whirl and which the death of a
friend forces renewed treatment, is that of Mariane, for whom
"Doris" once could playfully stand, but for whom now nothing more can stand. In working through his melancholy, in the
deepening of loss, the impossibility of holding on is reflected.
According to Haller's own 'theory of the trace,' the poem does
not collect old representations but rather deepens its traces
"after the stimulus (*Reiz*) has long gone."[33] A stimulus, one
might add, that bears no resemblance to the charm (*Reiz*) of
poetry. In the light of this theory, the apparent "charm of
light" vanishes, as is actually the case in the last stanza of the
Ode on Eternity.[34]

In the ode *On the Same,* Haller mentions yet another text
that he has dedicated to Mariane, the "stone that I have written—." He does not quote this text but marks it with a dash.
Its inscription ends with the following coda to Haller's name:
D Albertus Haller Med. Anat. Bot. P.P.O. *Hunc luge. Beata
lacrumis non eget.* There was nothing more to say. The insistent communicativity that was to be worked through in language is reduced to a formula chiseled in stone. While
obliquely related to the topic of epitaphs, it is directly related
to the Sermon on the Mount, whose wording it decomposes:
Beati, qui lugent: quoniam ipsi consolabuntur (Matthew, 5:4).
Consolation cannot be the subject here. The mourner is to be
mourned; the blessed needs no grief. Yet the point of this statement is not the orthodox prohibition against mourning but
rather the reflexion of enlightened mourning's melancholy
condition.

The intertextual references demonstrate not only a supposed immediacy as rhetorical effect; they demonstrate this
effect as part of a 'work on myth' whose vehicle is the text and
whose tenor is the reading of another text deposited in it. The
work of mourning on tradition, whose baroque, melancholy
disposition Haller's *Unfinished Ode* uncovers, is of no use to
the mourning whose work the text is meant to overcome. The
mourning aware of this impossibility has not exhausted the

schema of baroque melancholy in vain. The text that it leaves behind allows its enlightenment to be understood as the fulfillment of baroque intentions, not as their refutation. What Benjamin postulated as the deepening of mourning in baroque melancholy finds itself literarily completed only in its self-enlightenment. This occurs, however, at the cost of the poem, which, as empty form, is given up like a corpse to anatomy, while its contents, like the soul, are to be thought of elsewhere, in another place.

II. By The Figtree—Mnemosyne
(Hölderlin and Hegel)

Mnemosyne

Ein Zeichen sind wir, deutungslos
Schmerzlos sind wir und haben fast
Die Sprache in der Fremde verloren.
Wenn nemlich über Menschen
Ein Streit ist an dem Himmel und gewaltig
Die Monde gehn, so redet
Das Meer auch und Ströme müssen
Den Pfad sich suchen. Zweifellos
Ist aber Einer. Der
Kann täglich es ändern. Kaum bedarf er
Gesez. Und es tönet das Blatt und Eichbäume wehn
    dann neben
Den Firnen. Denn nicht vermögen
Die Himmlischen alles. Nemlich es reichen
Die Sterblichen eh' an den Abgrund. Also wendet es sich,
    das Echo
Mit diesen. Lang ist
Die Zeit, es ereignet sich aber
Das Wahre.

Wie aber liebes? Sonnenschein
Am Boden sehen wir und trokenen Staub
Und heimatlich die Schatten der Wälder und es blühet
An Dächern der Rauch, bei alter Krone
Der Thürme, friedsam; gut sind nemlich
Hat gegenredend die Seele
Ein Himmlisches verwundet, die Tageszeichen.
Denn Schnee, wie Majenblumen
Das Edelmüthige, wo
Es seie, bedeutend, glänzet auf
Der grünen Wiese
Der Alpen, hälftig, da, vom Kreuze redend, das
Gesezt ist unterwegs einmal
Gestorbenen, auf hoher Straß
Ein Wandersmann geht zornig,
Fern ahnend mit
Dem andern, aber was ist diß?

Am Feigenbaum ist mein
Achilles mir gestorben,
Und Ajax liegt
An den Grotten der See,
An Bächen, benachbart dem Skamandros.
An Schläfen Sausen einst, nach
Der unbewegten Salamis steter
Gewohnheit, in der Fremd', ist groß
Ajax gestorben
Patroklos aber in des Königes Harnisch. Und es starben
Noch andere viel. Am Kithäron aber lag
Elevterä, der Mnemosyne Stadt. Der auch als
Ablegte den Mantel Gott, das abendliche nachher löste
Die Loken. Himmlische nemlich sind
Unwillig, wenn einer nicht die Seele schonend sich
Zusammengenommen, aber er muß doch; dem
Gleich fehlet die Trauer.

Mnemosyne

A sign we are, without interpretation
Without pain we are and have almost
Lost our language in foreign parts.
For when above, over humans,
War is in heaven and forcefully
Moons proceed, the sea
Responds also and rivers must find
Their way. But no doubt
There is One. He
Can change this any day. Hardly needs he
A law. But then, leaves sound and thus oak trees blow
Beside the still frozen snow. Because not everything
Is in the power of those in heaven. Anyway
Mortals, namely, border on the abyss. So it returns,
The echo, with them. It takes a long
Time, but what comes true is
The truth.

How, however, does love come true? Sunshine
We see on the ground and dry dust
And woods deep with shadows and there blooms
Smoke on the roofs, near the old crowns
Of towers, peaceful; for they are good,
The signs of the day, if in response
Something heavenly has wounded the soul.
For snow, like May flowers,
Signifying something noble, where
It is, gleams on the green meadow
Of the Alps, in part,
There, talking of the cross,
Placed for those who once
Died on their way, high up
A traveler walks raging,

From far intimating
The other, but what is it?

By the figtree it happened to me
My Achilles died,
And Ajax lies
By the grottoes of the sea,
By streams, close to the Skamandros,
Of a roar in his temples, at the end
Of the unmoved Salamis' persisting
Custom, in foreign parts, great
Ajax died.
But Patroklos, he died in the king's armor. And
Others died, many. But near Kithairon lay
Eleutherai, city of Mnemosyne. Also she,
When God put down his mantle, evening loosened
Her locks. For the heavenly are
Angry if someone has not, saving himself,
Pulled together his soul, but still he must; for him
However the mourning is missing.

Stanza I, second version
Stanzas II–III, third version

[Chadwick's translation]

Hölderlin's last line, the last line of his last hymn, *Mnemosyne*, appears at first and even second glance hardly problematic. There is almost complete agreement that in this line mourning is not simply missing but rather is at fault. Since Friedrich Beissner first edited the poem in the *Hölderlin Jahrbuch* of 1948–49, his first reading has remained almost uncontested: "Mourning . . . errs like the one who failed to restrain himself and roused the anger of the Heavenly. Mourning commits the same error as this one in that it also lets itself slip without resistance into death."[1] Even Sattler, who seldom misses an opportunity to question Beissner's edition, takes pains to protect what seems beyond question for the experienced Hölderlin scholar: "According to ordinary language *gleich* could be misunderstood as *sofort* [immediately] and *fehlt* as *nicht vorhanden* [not present]. The mourning for the deceased thus corresponds to the 'sin' of the wish to die."[2] Indeed, according to the grammar of this difficult poem, nothing seems simpler than the conclusion: "but still he must"; that is, he who "has not, saving himself, pulled together his soul," and likewise, nonetheless, must die. "Like him, mourning is at fault" in precisely the sense that it is not present. The rare unanimity of Hölderlin interpreters, not satisfied with mere 'lack' and insisting on the weightier 'erring' of mourning, gives evidence of a peculiar blindness (as Paul de Man would say) that confirms the questionable state of affairs *ex negativo*, in the denial.

In both Sattler's compact summary and Beissner's commentary, the phrase *dem/Gleich* has no such temporal implications but rather signifies a pure 'correspondence' in error: the failed collection of the soul and the failed mourning. What is striking about this especially crude equation is the exemplary conclusion that it draws, as if it were a matter of objective knowledge of the kind expressed by the imperative: "Pull yourself together!"[3] Only separated by a semicolon, the supplementary remark of *Mnemosyne—dem/Gleich fehlet die Trauer*—appears to be an intensification of a thought in the previous main clause. The poet adds an afterthought of which it is uncertain whether it is suited for reinforcing the intention of the main thought (the "anger" of the Heavenly) or—as in the manner of afterthoughts—for undermining it and putting it into question.

That *fehlet* according to Hölderlin's vocabulary here only means *fehlgehen* (erring, going astray), as Böschenstein's concordance affirms,[4] raises the question: how else, if not by its absence, could *fehlen* err? Not contrary to linguistic usage but rather according to its provisions (one could contend) does that other Hölderlinian signification achieve its significance. One may say more precisely that what is essential to the development of this significance is Hölderlin's preference for the etymological origins of language rather than its ordinary uses.[5] Mourning's error is grounded in the absence of mourning and consists in nothing but its lack. Freud's treatment of this state of affairs is no different: "melancholy appears in the place of mourning."[6] For the missing mourning a faulty mourning steps in, one that carries the name of melancholia.

"By the figtree it happened to me/My Achilles died . . . " Beissner designates these two lines "the germ of the poem."[7] Even if the genetic argument is fallacious, it provides a useful myth that reconciles the poetics of *Mnemosyne* with its origination and, beginning with its last stanza, permits it to be read anew from last to first. Like the last sentence—*dem/ Gleich fehlet die Trauer*—the last stanza of the poem also recasts the preceding verses, retrospectively setting the end at the beginning by showing the beginning as the end. This is the movement of the myth that is remembered, the beginning that returns at the end: the Homeric epic of the wrath of Achilles ("Muse sing the fatal wrath of the Pelide, Achilles," in Hölderlin's own translation). Thus the question that ends the second stanza—"A traveler walks raging/From far intimating/The other, but what is this?"—finds its answer in the third. The critical commonplace of Hölderlin's identification with Achilles, which has been played out on all levels by Hölderlin studies, experiences in this connection an essential modification. The lyrical 'I,' of which the double use of the personal pronoun reminds us (*mein Achilles mir*), does not merely show, as Beissner phrases it, an "intimate concern for the heroic figure of youth." Rather, it bears witness to an identification through wrath that results at the end of the third stanza in the inability to mourn.

The remembrance of myth is directed towards its "wrathful heroes" (*zorn'gen Helden*, as in the ode entitled *Thränen*). Even more than the death of Achilles, it pertains to the suicide of Ajax, whose anger had been inflamed by the loss of the "king's armor" to the cunning Odysseus. The subject here is not the survivor but the death of the others ("And/Others died, many.").[8] With the prototypical wrath of Achilles and his glorious death the archaic anger of Ajax and his ignominious suicide are brought into tragic perspective. Furthermore, it is not the case that Hölderlin's poem amounts to a cataloguing of traditional details like the figtree, metonymic landmark of the battlefield of Troy, or Salamis, the island of Ajax. This peculiar arbitrariness of detail does not depend on the associative connection of names nor does it represent scenes from the epic. What the positivist research into such details contributes to this stanza (I refer here chiefly to Beissner and Jochen Schmidt) are objects of myth that are not yet per se objects of poems. The referential code of such commentary reduces a dimension of intertextual exchange that is already registered in that same commentary and in that same code.

Hölderlin thus repeats here his reading of the heroic myths of classical Greece and does so not in the enumeration of references but in the wording of his own translations. He does not recollect the epic so much as seek a recollective appropriation of epic. In addition to the figtree from the *Iliad* and Pausanias's reference to the city of Mnemosyne (direct references), this passage has to do above all with quotations from the *Ajax* of Sophocles and Pindar, especially the second *Nemean Ode*.[9] Here it is noteworthy how Pindar's scheme, that is, the derivation of the hero from his home (Ajax from Salamis), is fulfilled and surpassed by the Sophoclean monologue (in *Ajax*). Pindar writes: "and truly she, the Salamis ["the unmoved Salamis" of *Mnemosyne*] was able to rear a man deadly in battle. Before the walls of Troy, Hektor learned this from Ajax." In Sophocles this same man, calling to his distant Salamis, succumbs to madness and ends in suicide.

In his reconstruction of Hölderlin's theory of the "modulation of tones," Szondi has worked out a progression towards 'epicization' in the thesis: "the *perfection* [*Vollendung*] of the lyric lies in the epic."[10] Yet *Mnemosyne* shows that such an insertion of epic passages into the lyrical poem works in the service not so much of a return of the epic as of its renewed remembrance in precarious circumstances. "The tendency towards the epic in the lyrical as well as the tragic poem," for which Szondi adduces both Pindar's seventh *Olympian Ode* and Sophocles' *Ajax*, becomes in *Mnemosyne* itself historical:

Hölderlin cites it as a failed attempt. What Szondi calls, in Hölderlin's phrase, "the *epic* treatment" of the lyrical poem goes beyond the modulation of tones and lies also outside tri-adic ('dialectical') construction. (I will not go any further into this here.) Agreeing with Beissner's hypothesis about the ori-gin of the poem, Szondi calls the "naive" tone of epic style the "germcell of the representational mode that characterizes, throughout and ever more exclusively, Hölderlin's late works." Following early remarks by Benjamin, Adorno gave this naive-epic mode of representation in late Hölderlin the name 'paratactic,' and therein identified in particular its metonymic character. More precise than Jakobson's charac-terization of the epic ('narrative') in terms of metonomy, Adorno's parataxis signifies a "resistance to synthesis" that rests more on a grammatical than a semantical opposition of the para- vs. the syntactic. That is what he means when he says that "in Hölderlin the poetic movement upsets for the first time the category of meaning."[11] Parataxis undermines the synthetic accomplishments of syntax that make the boundaries of synthesis legible. It is Adorno's contention that, in the paratactic countermovement to the syntactic produc-tion of meaning (more precisely, parataxis vs. hypotaxis), lan-guage does not lead "beyond the subject" but rather speaks "for the subject . . . which can no longer speak (Hölderlin was probably the first whose art had some idea of this) from out of itself" (Adorno's parentheses).

Thus the concept of parataxis has more than the descrip-tive uses Szondi finds in it. The paratactic sequence of mythic elements in the last stanza of *Mnemosyne* is a case in point. In Benjamin's formulation, on which both Adorno and Szondi rely, "Men, the Heavenly, and princes" seem to "fall headlong out of their old orders into sheer contiguity [*zueinander gereiht*]."[12] The fall out of the old order of things into metonymic arbitrariness, that is, from the syntax of the order of things into the parataxis of a text that no longer represents, or corresponds to, the order of things, is in *Mnemosyne* no fall of figures and names but of texts whose wreckage results in a ghostly after-image of that which was once to be epically remembered as myth. Pausanias's description of the ruins of "Eleutherai," whose name is superimposed on the "fields of Mnemosyne" as handed down from Hesiod, is the allegory suited to this state of affairs. "But near Kithairon lay/Eleutherai, city of Mnemosyne."

In this sentence, which first brings the title of the poem into play, two texts are projected, one on top of the other.[13] In Hesiod's *Theogony* appears the notorious verses about the mother of the muses ("ruling over the fields of Eleutherai"), to which Pausanias adds the historical localization of a devastated city: already in antiquity the "city of Mnemosyne" was a ruin. Its name, "Eleutherai" (freedom), signifies with extreme irony what remains to be deciphered as the cultural trace in mythic nature. Of this Benjamin's statement holds true: "On the face of nature 'History' is written in the ciphers of the vanishing past."[14] The ciphers of the vanishing past are all that remains readable in the disappearance of Eleutherai. The history to which this devastation testifies and the myth that it helps to localize have become unreadable. It remains readable only as an allegory of the unreadability of its "vanishing past" (*Vergängnis* in Benjamin).

In one of Hölderlin's fragments, the problematic of which will not be quickly exhausted by our reading, we find first a speculative, then a rhetorical definition of the lyric: "The lyrical and, according to sensuous appearance [*dem Schein nach*], ideal poem is naive in its meaning. It is a continuous metaphor of *one* feeling."[15] In the rhetorical lexicon still common in Hölderlin's day (the *continua metaphora* of Quintilian), the lyrical poem is conceived of as an allegory whose coherence guarantees the unity of a single feeling. Since the lyrical poem is, in Hölderlin's definition, the ideal poem according to sensuous appearance and is naive in its meaning, this allegory elevates a naive meaning to the appearance of the ideal. In the tendency of the late hymns, as interpreted by Szondi, the ideal appearance of the "art character" (*Kunstcharakter*) of the poem turns naive: the lyrical poem becomes epic. The naive "ground" (*Grund*), however, turns heroic: wrath becomes mourning. Yet this last turn, according to Hölderlin's last verse, fails. The naive meaning of the unity of one feeling of wrath, whose extended metaphor replaces the allegory of history in the ideal appearance of epic, refuses to be recast in the heroic meaning of mourning. Such "allegories," the rhetorical commonplace crucial to the work of Paul de Man, "are always allegories of metaphor and, as such, they are always allegories of the impossibility of reading."[16] Not accidentally does de Man come or, better, remain so near Hölderlin in the center of his theory. The inability to mourn results from an impossibility to read: in Hölderlin the naive "ground" of wrath becomes, in the extended metaphor that history unfolds, the allegory of an unreadability whose mourning remains melancholia. Wrath remains unreadable as metaphor ('tenor') of the naive "art character" ('vehicle') and, as the metaphor of the naive "ground" ('meaning') that has become unreadable, its lyrical development becomes the allegory of a failure.[17] Mimetic affinity with the anger of the hero ("From far intimating/The other . . . ") turns into what Adorno calls "mimetic affinity with death"—the death of Mnemosyne.[18]

The extreme radicalization of the third version of *Mnemosyne* occurs in the shift from the "wild courage" and "divine force" of heroes, which was the subject of the previous versions, to the death of memory itself, Mnemosyne: "Also she,/When God put down his mantle, evening loosened/ Her locks." Hölderlin communicates this unheard-of event, which is something entirely his own, in the words in which another modern, Schiller, translates another ancient author, Virgil. Beissner discovered the wording in the later version of Schiller's *Dido*, dating from 1803, the same year as *Mnemosyne*.[19] In the context of the story of Dido, the undoing of the tresses (*Lösen der Locken*) as well as the laying down of the mantle have romantic overtones that associate the tragic *Liebestod* with the consummation of the love act. A characteristic example of this would be Keats's *Ode on Melancholy*, about which Empson said: "it pounds together the sensations of joy and sorrow till they combine into sexuality."[20] In *Mnemosyne* a fusion of this kind is recalled and reversed. Its lyrical tone, through the epicization of the poem from the

Iliad to the *Aeneid,* is colored "naive" in order that it may fail "sentimentally." The romantic possibility that would draw from melancholy a temporary and as such questionable pleasure (one that Keats pushes to the extreme) is never a serious consideration for Hölderlin and is rejected. The final incapacity of mourning is made manifest by the death of Mnemosyne. It exhausts the possibilities of the lyric in that it grounds the impossibility of reading in the inability to mourn. As a motif, this death is not comparable with the vanishing of the muses that made such an excellent pretext for lyrical melancholy in the elegiac tradition up to the Göttinger Hain.[21] The loss of mourning signifies the loss of all the "defense mechanisms of understanding," as de Man has remarked: the loss of the ability "to collect the soul, to save it."[22]

It is interesting that Hölderlin takes the death of Mnemosyne, which cannot be quoted from any other text, from the mouth of another and indeed none other than Schiller. He abandons Schiller in order to turn one last time to what de Man has recognized as his adaptation of Rousseau: "the 'one' designated in these lines ["if someone has not, saving himself,/Pulled together his soul . . . "] can be none other than Rousseau."[23] The formulation is contradictory, however, for this "one" is no one in the quoted passage and remains none. Even Hölderlin fails in the face of Rousseau's demand. And yet this demand fits no one else but Rousseau. In the phrase "to re-collect oneself" (*sich zusammennehmen*) "re-collection" happily entails a prior "collection" (*Sammlung*), which Hölderlin interpreted as "preservation" (*Schonung*). Hölderlin almost quotes the stanza of his Rhine hymn dedicated to Rousseau: "But he whose soul, like yours, Rousseau,/Ever strong and patient/Became invincible. . . . "[24] Böschenstein identified the relevant passage from Rousseau's fifth *Rêverie*: "But it is a state where the soul finds a place firm enough for complete repose and can assemble its entire being without having need of recalling the past or glancing to the future."[25] Yet the image of Rousseau survives merely as an image and functions in *Mnemosyne* only as a quotation, as an instance of heavenly "anger" (*Unwillen*) against which there is no appeal. What remains to the poet, who had identified himself with the wrath of Achilles and now faces the destiny of Ajax, is only a final remark—*dem/Gleich fehlet die Trauer.*

The failure of appropriation that manifests itself in the remembrance of the Greeks nevertheless practices a self-recollection within the text of the poem. The result of this recollection, however, loses that which is collected. *Der Grübler,* we read in Benjamin's fragments, *dessen Blick, auf-geschreckt, auf das Bruchstück in seiner Hand fällt, wird zum Allegoriker.*—"Lost in melancholy, the brooder turns allegoric, when all of a sudden he realizes that the piece in his hand is a fragment."[26] Epic parataxis does not reconstitute the epic but rather collects the fragments of its appropriation so as to become in them shockingly aware of the loss. The allegorical coherence of *Mnemosyne* consists in nothing more than this metonymic accumulation of its parts that does not represent the myth itself so much as its loss in the process of futile appropriation. This poem is itself only insofar as it presents others as itself.

Hölderlin interpretation, especially under Heidegger's imprimatur, has also sought to discover some "savior" (*Rettendes*) here—"where danger threatens salvation also grows." Thus, *Was bleibet aber, stiften die Dichter* are the last words of the poem *Andenken* whose covert relationship with *Mnemosyne* would be worthwhile to investigate. It would appear that the power of remembrance (*Andenken*) to save is proportionate to that of the death of Mnemosyne to threaten.[27] Such may have been a possible interpretation of the earlier versions of Hölderlin's poem, but in the third version the death of Mnemosyne does not merely threaten. Rather, it is already decreed. This prior completion is what Dieter Henrich aptly formulated as the difference between Hegel and Hölderlin: "For Hegel, to remember [*Erinnern*] is always to transform: interiorization [*Er-innerung*] as the overcoming of the past's being-in-itself. . . . For Hölderlin, on the contrary, memory is a preserving [*Bewahren*] that stands under the claim to be true to the past and hence seeks and maintains the past in its own right."[28] The mythic organ of interiorization in Hegel is the epic singer whose "pathos is not the stupefying power of nature, but Mnemosyne, recollection [*Besinnung*] and developed inwardness, the interiorization [*Erinnerung*] of the once immediate essence."[29] Being true to this no longer immediate essence turns the preservation of the past into an impossible endeavor. De Man's last essay on "Anthropomorphism and Trope in the Lyric" gives to this aporia its last, deconstructive variation. The lyric turns into a "paradigm of represented voice" by means of a "transformation of trope into anthropomorphism."[30] The traditionally understood lyrical I of a poem organizes the poetic figures of the text, its allegory, into an anthropomorphism that represents "the illusionary resuscitation of the natural breath of language, frozen into stone by the semantic power of the trope." Similarly, Hegel's Mnemosyne appears in Hölderlin as something that has long been entrusted to death. The frozen allegory, which appears in *Mnemosyne* in the fragments of intertextual references, restores no epic muse. At best, epic parataxis recalls mimetic naiveté without yet being able to demonstrate anything other than the failure of this mimesis. It is the failure of the anthropomorphism of the (lyrically represented) voice to represent the voice of the epic muse.

Melancholy, in other words, is to the anthropomorphism of the lyric as irony is to that of the novel. This becomes true once 'the melancholy of the muses,' which is the subject of Burton's *Anatomy*, is superseded by the invocation of the Muse Melancholia. Next to irony, which has been taken since Quintilian's double definition as both trope and state of mind (Socrates being its personification), melancholy becomes the predominant anthropomorphism of trope. *Mnemosyne* is not simply an allegory of the lyric; rather it shows the latter in the state of melancholy. The death of Mnemosyne reduces melancholy to its allegorical denominator. On its 'face,' to recall Benjamin's image, 'Allegory' is written in the ciphers of the vanishing past. Under the sign of Allegory, however, reading remains melancholy and does not meet the condition of 'true' mourning (where true mourning means being true to that which preserves). The anthropomorphic tenor of this allegory proves, as de Man emphasizes, that "the possibility of anthropomorphic (mis)reading is part of the text and part of what is at stake in it."[31] In a way more attentive to 'content,' one can thus describe melancholy as the 'mood' of a lyrical I and its attitude to the subject matter of the poem.

Now one can certainly not say, however, that Hölderlin, of whose late, almost baroque phase Benjamin speaks, succumbs to baroque melancholy (nor does this have anything to do with his psychiatric diagnosis). On the contrary, it is his resistance—his mourning, to be more precise—that leads him 'beyond the subject.' "In the late hymns," Adorno continues in the passage already quoted, "subjectivity is not the absolute and not the ultimate. It is understood rather to commit a sacrilege in which it imposes itself as if it were absolute and ultimate, all the while following an inner logic of self-positing. This is the construction of *hubris* in Hölderlin."[32] In *Mnemosyne*, the sacrilege of hubristic subjectivity is the anthropomorphism of the lyrical I that invokes objects the interiorization (*Er-innerung*) of which follows the logic of melancholic self-positing. The second stanza of the poem had opened with a question: *Wie aber liebes?*—"How, however [if ever], does love come true?" This question presupposes the syntactic construction of a statement with which the first stanza had ended and which is thus put into question (or made relative to it) by the second: *es ereignet sich aber/Das Wahre*— "what is true is what is bound to take place" in de Man's translation.[33] With this syntactic construction in mind, the question at the beginning of the second stanza reads as a question of whether love is bound to take place: *Wie aber ereignet sich liebes?* (Insofar as the word *ereignet* does not appear in Hölderlin's text, it becomes clear that *liebes* will accordingly not take place.)

Under this question Hölderlin's "traveler" walks along the heights of the Alps, the boundary between the Hesperides and the Greek south. "From far intimating/The other," he identifies with his hero in wrath. In his *Notes to Oedipus*, Hölderlin treated wrath as the moment of identification in tragedy that, as a "limitless unification" of God and man, in-

ner and outer nature, is to be purified by "limitless separation."[34] The wrath of the traveler in *Mnemosyne* is motivated
by the compulsion to achieve such a limitless unification, yet
is simultaneously characterized by the futility of such striv-
ing. This wrath is no longer the result of a naive identification
with the hero but rather is dominated by the failure of the
compulsion to imitate. Just as Dante's wanderer succumbs, in
a momentary identification, to Francesca's seductive talent, a
weakness that completes itself in a mimetic swoon, so Hölderlin's wanderer is overwhelmed by the wrath of his hero
Achilles, whom he repeats in the text in a mimesis as com-
pulsive as it is helpless.[35]

The loss of the first figure of identification leaves him
with the role of "the second best Achaean," Ajax.[36] For the latter was not only second after Achilles but, moreover, was one
who already had failed in the attempt to replace Achilles' sur-
rogate and alter ego, Patroklos, who had died "in the king's armor." Ajax is the negative reflection of Achilles as Patroklos
is the positive. He fails to occupy the place of Achilles, both in
the role of the first among heroes and in his coveted armor,
which he loses to Odysseus. The anger of Ajax, which does not
match the wrath of Achilles but remains limited to its imitation, turns into ridiculous madness when he—caricature of
the wrathful hero—mistakes a herd of cattle for the enemy
army.[37] At least one further passage from the context of
Hölderlin's translation of Sophocles should be mentioned. Beside the "grottoes of the sea," the moribund Ajax imagines the
hard, relentless complaint of his mother, "when of his sickness,/his madness she hears."[38] The rage of the mother motivates his suicide.

Indeed, it seems to have been the question of the mother
rather than the father that was crucial for Hölderlin's own fate,
which in *Mnemosyne*, as Helm Stierlin has remarked, "expresses a despair beyond despair—that is, that state of mind
which, so it seems, allows only for suicide or massive schizophrenic disintegration and retreat."[39] The psychological diagnosis has here a significance that is not external to the text. It
draws our attention to a structure similar to a double bind that

links the impossible appropriation of the Greeks with their impossible allegory and impossible mourning: *dem/Gleich fehlet die Trauer* represents this double bind that the reader seeks to circumvent only to succumb to it all the more certainly. While complaining about errors in mourning, the reader lacks it in himself to the same extent that he denies it. He succumbs to the inability to mourn as Hölderlin succumbs to the wrath of his hero. In this case, the meaning of re-presentation is determined by a repetition on the side of the reader, on the receiving end. If such a thing is conceivable as a "fundamental division in the writer's mind," as Empson claims for the seventh of his *Seven Types of Ambiguity*, its consideration of representability in the text would be its reenactment in the reader's mind.[40] The anthropomorphism of represented voice, as it were, has as its echo an anthropomorphism of reception: the 'subjectivity' of the reader. His subjectivity is, in Hölderlin's words, nothing but the 'echo' of lyrical melancholy.

Melencholia illa heroica is an expression by Melanchthon whose tradition suits Hölderlin as well as Baudelaire, whom Benjamin studied in relation to this tradition.[41] In heroism vis-à-vis the temptations of melancholy—not yet to the extent of 'spleen' but certainly in their scorn for *süße Melancholey*—Hölderlin and Baudelaire are close. Hölderlin's heroic measure, indeed, lies not in any identification with the hero's wrath, but in the endurance of an impossible mourning, which distantly grieves for the loss of an 'other' who assumes his own features in the appropriation of the past that occurs in reading. In the impossibility of this mourning, *Andenken*, the title of the poem to which *Mnemosyne*'s title evidently refers, becomes the contemplation (*Nachdenken*) of a mnemonic trace, which the erection of the other as hero has left behind. It is marked through mnemonic signs the encounter of which triggers vain feelings: "talking of the cross,/Placed for those who once/Died on their way," arouses the anger of the traveler in his "distant intimation" of the (lost) other. The equivalent of this cross in the Homeric epic alluded to in the third stanza is the figtree, in which ancient and Christian tradition (anamnesis and anagogy) intersect in the manner of a chiasmus: the cross stands for the death of this life, while the figtree is the reminder of a promised afterlife (for which various passages in the *New Testament* could be cited, in particular Augustine's *Confessions*).

In Augustine, the *conversio* takes place under such a figtree, in Petrarch, who in the *Secretum* sees himself reminded of Augustine's tree, the subject is rememembrance, whose sign the figtree is. What the testimony of Petrarch here points out is the sign character of this tree for the remembrance of remembrance (*Andenken der Erinnerung*). The figtree in *Mnemosyne* would thus stand, as a reminiscence of that which is remembered in *Andenken*, for the cross: in Augustine for the sign of the cross of baptism, in Hölderlin for the wayside cross of the 'other.' Yet it is not the case that this sign of death in *Mnemosyne* is replaced with a sign of promise. On the contrary, this other sign recalls the failure of the other remembrance, a failure to which this other remembrance succumbs as well. If the figtree in *Andenken* stands for remembrance, then it stands in *Mnemosyne* for the impossibility also of this remembrance that is *Andenken*.

In the second stanza of *Andenken* the figtree is set apart from the other trees: "But in the courtyard a figtree grows." Sattler, who reads all these trees as memorials (the oak tree for Klopstock, a silver poplar for Heinse), identifies the figtree as Diotima, whose destiny has fulfilled itself in its sign ("I will be" are her last words in *Hyperion*).[42] The examples are problematic in detail, but it is not difficult to derive from them the figtree as a double sign for Achilles and Diotima, hero and beloved. It is noteworthy that in the case of this hero the incommensurable wrath is inflamed by the loss of his beloved (Briseis), at which point his mother comes to his aid (a mother whose absence Hölderlin bewails in the elegy *Achill*). Hence the figtree in *Mnemosyne* seems to stand as echo of that which is remembered in *Andenken*, i.e. the cross. But it is not the case that the sign of death is simply replaced by the sign of promise. On the contrary, this other sign is reminiscent of the failure of another remembrance, but this reminiscence fails as well. If the figtree in *Andenken* triggers recollection, then it

stands in *Mnemosyne* also for the impossibility of this recollection. The symbol of the beloved gets absorbed into the sign
of the hero whose futile imitation had raised her to a symbol
in whose imitation she herself had succumbed to death. The
promise in death, not the death in promise, is *aufgehoben*
(both cancelled and preserved). In that it symbolizes the failure of interiorization, the figtree signifies mourning. The place
of death (the grave, as many would have it) of the failed hero
(Achilles under the figtree) becomes a sign of mourning for the
lost love outside the poem (not Diotima but Susette). She does
not lack mourning, nor does the poet lack her. His poem has
the structure of a krypt *through* which (not *in* which) a loss is
preserved and concealed. This is what is signified through the
poem and what remains readable in the 'error' of the poem:
"The 'recounted' event, reconstructed through a novelistic
and mythic-dramatic-poetic genesis, never appears."[43] It does
not appear in the story of the poem but occurs through the epicization of the lyric and its paratactic failure.

 *Ein Zeichen sind wir, deutungslos/Schmerzlos sind wir
und haben fast/Die Sprache in der Fremde verloren.*—"A sign
we are, without interpretation/Without pain we are and have
almost/Lost our language in foreign parts." The third and last
version of the third stanza of *Mnemosyne* still presupposes
this first stanza of the second version (the third version of the
first stanza in Beissner's reconstruction being of a later date).
What remains of our language are signs without interpretation. What the poets establish is not interpretation but the
assurance that the signs remain. *Stiften*, etymologically, suggests the 'stiffening' of the sign.[44] What does not remain,
what is dismissed, on the other hand, is the anger and pain
transmitted by interpretation. The transmission occurs in an
echo—mentioned by Hölderlin in the same stanza (second version) as the lines quoted above—an echo that characterizes
the relation between mortals and gods. Indeed, the echo is the
perfect allegory of divine anthropomorphism (of anthropomorphism *par excellence*): it does not answer, but sounds deceptively like an answer.[45] It is, in other words, the allegory
of mimesis as deception (*Täuschung*). What the poets estab-

lish in the anthropomorphism of the lyrical voice is what remains in the sign after all disappointment (*Enttäuschung*).
What leads Hölderlin beyond subjectivity is the un-deception
(*Ent-täuschung*), or de-construction, of the human as echo,
of lyrical melancholy as anthropomorphism. The death of
Mnemosyne, therefore, signifies no end. The sentence of Hesiod's *Theogony* that calls her the mother of the muses also
gives the latter's part of the story. It is the opposite of their
mother's name, forgetting of ills and a cessation of anxieties.[46]
The death of Mnemosyne dissolves the effort of *lesmosyne*
and brings a return of the repressed: through signs symptoms,
not symbols, traces not tropes.

III. Secluded Laurel—Andenken
(Hölderlin and Heidegger)

Andenken

Der Nordost wehet,
Der liebste unter den Winden
Mir, weil er feurigen Geist
Und gute Fahrt verheißet den Schiffern.
Geh aber nun und grüße
Die schöne Garonne,
Und die Gärten von Bourdeaux
Dort, wo am scharfen Ufer
Hingehet der Steg und in den Strom
Tief fällt der Bach, darüber aber
Hinschauet ein edel Paar
Von Eichen und Silberpappeln;

Noch denket das mir wohl und wie
Die breiten Gipfel neiget
Der Ulmwald, über die Mühl',
Im Hofe aber wächset ein Feigenbaum.
An Feiertagen gehn
Die braunen Frauen daselbst

Auf seidnen Boden,
Zur Märzenzeit,
Wenn gleich ist Nacht und Tag,
Und über langsamen Stegen,
Von goldenen Träumen schwer,
Einwiegende Lüfte ziehen.

Es reiche aber,
Des dunkeln Lichtes voll,
Mir einer den duftenden Becher,
Damit ich ruhen möge; denn süß
Wär' unter Schatten der Schlummer.
Nicht ist es gut,
Seellos von sterblichen
Gedanken zu seyn. Doch gut
Ist ein Gespräch und zu sagen
Des Herzens Meinung, zu hören viel
Von Tagen der Lieb',
Und Thaten, welche geschehen.

Wo aber sind die Freunde? Bellarmin
Mit den Gefährten? Mancher
Trägt Scheue, an die Quelle zu gehen;
Es beginnet nemlich der Reichtum
Im Meere. Sie,
Wie Mahler, bringen zusammen
Das Schöne der Erd' und verschmähn
Den geflügelten Krieg nicht, und
Zu wohnen einsam, jahrlang, unter
Dem enlaubten Mast, wo nicht die Nacht durchglänzen
Die Feiertage dcr Stadt,
Und Saitenspiel und eingeborener Tanz nicht.

Nun aber sind zu Indiern
Die Männer gegangen,
Dort an der luftigen Spiz'
An Traubenbergen, wo herab
Die Dordogne kommt,

Und zusammen mit der prächt'gen
Garonne meerbreit
Ausgehet der Strom. Es nehmet aber
Und giebt Gedächtniß die See,
Und die Lieb' auch heftet fleißig die Augen,
Was bleibet aber, stiften die Dichter.

Souvenir

The nor'easter blows,
The favorite among winds
To me, since it promises firey spirit
And safe passage to sailors.
But go now and greet
The lovely Garonne
And the gardens of Bordeaux,
There, where along the sharp cove
Trails the path and into the river
Deep dives the stream, but over it
Looks out a noble pair
Of oaks and silver poplars;

It still comes back to me how
The broad tops of the elm wood
Bend over the mill,
But in the courtyard a figtree grows.
On holidays there
Brown women walk
On silky ground,
At Marchtide,
When equal are night and day,
And over tranquil paths
Heavy with golden dreams,
Drift lulling breezes.

But someone should pass,
Full of dark light,

That fragrant cup to me,
That I might rest; for sweet
Would be slumber under shadows.
It's not good
To be without the soul
Of mortal thought. Because
Conversation is good and to speak
The heart's meaning, to hear much
Of days of love
And deeds that happened.

But where are the friends? Bellarmin
And the companions? Some
Are reluctant to go to the source;
Namely, wealth begins
At sea. They,
Like painters, bring together
The beauty of the earth, nor shun
Wings of war or
To live alone, years long, beneath
The denuded mast, where night is not brightened
By the holidays of the city,
Not by lyre or native dance.

But now for the Indians
The men have left
From the breezy cape
Near the vineyards, from where
The Dordogne descends
And together with the majestic
Garonne, as wide as the ocean,
The river leaves. But it takes
And gives memory the sea,
And also love is busy fixing the eyes,
But what remains, establish the poets.

[Chadwick's translation]

Hölderlin was not rediscovered without the help of philosophers, nor since this discovery, which freed him from the rank of a minor romantic, has he been read without philosophical interest. But Hölderlin research has been able to disengage itself from the—at times more or less ideologically colored—premises of its philosophical interest in knowledge only where it has specialized in poetological questions, thereby raising Hölderlin from proto-philosopher to exemplary theoretician of poetry. In questions of interpretation one has remained dependent on the theoretical odds of a more general or a more particular kind—with what right, this is the question that, from Dilthey up to Dieter Henrich, arises from the background of Hegelian philosophy.

Andenken, whose philosophical title more than its poetic contents has held a position next to, if not equal with, the great hymns of the late work, has been promoted, by way of the philosophical and poetological problematizations in the evolution of Hölderlin studies, to one of the best known of Hölderlin's poems. This rests not least with Heidegger's fundamental interpretation, which up to the present day has remained definitive, so that one could say that the success of this poem is itself a chapter in the history of the reception of Heidegger's thought. The editor of the *Große Stuttgarter Ausgabe* begins his "Elucidations" to *Andenken* with a single, laconic observation whose consequence seems to need no further elucidation: "Martin Heidegger uses the poem as an occasion to develop his philosophy"[1]—a sentence not without critical undertone, yet also not without pride in the role played by the poem in this 'development' and in any case without resistance to its overbearing demand. In many respects, the newest monograph by Dieter Henrich, *On the Road to Andenken*, represents the antithesis to this demand. It intends to restore to this poem, which Heidegger reduced to a pretext of his philosophy, a poetical dimension that, according to Henrich, deserves to be taken into account by philosophers. On the last page of his book Henrich calls it a "philosophical" poem because—in contrast to the hymn *Mnemosyne*, for example—

it is "nearer to the tone in which philosophy achieves and clarifies its insight."[2] However, this relation of 'tones' (already a Hölderlinian metaphor) itself requires clarification. In it is harbored the mutuality of an insight that owes nothing to philosophical supposition but rather "can be completed only in the thought of the poem."

What makes *Andenken* exemplary, what qualifies it as an exemplary crux of philosophical reading, manifests itself in Henrich's reading sharpened, purified of one-sided suppositions, yet with the same aporetical consequence that Paul de Man already criticized in Heidegger's reading of the poem and raised to the performative contradiction of *Blindness and Insight*: "Hölderlin says exactly the contrary of what Heidegger makes him say."[3] The point, in its pointedness, needs elaborating. For, in the case of Henrich, one cannot say that a philosopher has "imputed" the opposite of what the poet had to say. On the contrary: what was misunderstood by Heidegger in its historical circumstances and was turned into the powerful pretext of his own thought—Hölderlin's poem—receives with Henrich the subtlest reconstruction from the idealist text milieu from which it arose. But insofar as Henrich reconstructs what the poem presupposes in terms of philosophy, he interprets only one side of what the poem actually is (as a poem). Calling on a well-known formulation of Valéry ("concerning the subject of *Cimetière marin*"), Henrich reads (as he says in the following passage, in explicit connection with Heidegger's idiom) what "can be *completed* in the thought of the poem"; but he does not read the completion of this thinking in and along with the poem—a completion that, in the present case, experiences a collapse of the same thinking. One might say that Henrich neglects, if ironically only to follow Hölderlin's thought (what Heidegger takes from Hölderlin as 'thinking of'), that which Hölderlin 'performs' in his text.

Valéry's emphasis on 'poetic construction' is of course only partially clarifying, and de Man has occasionally warned against an 'over-valéryzation' of poetics. Likewise is this warning only the other side of the same problem, the very same that de Man expressed through Hölderlin as "the obvious stumbling block of my [his] own enterprise," and this not only in view of his collection of early Hölderlin studies (on which he has commented with this preliminary remark) but more in view of a possible, though unwritten, book that would have taken Hölderlin as the paradigm of deconstruction.[4] Nevertheless, with the aid of de Man's Heidegger critique a problem can be situated whose return in Henrich's book occurs on a new, now also philologically more secure level and demands now a new, philologically more appropriate answer. Philological security, however, is here the least of problems, whose solution has to be thought through always again. The problem is in no way only one of the securing of re-constructions but rather of a conflict of readings. It does not arise naturally out of philological operations but in fact guides them; thus—and more essentially—it is also a problem of the inscribed, non-constructed, resistant element of all constructions.[5]

Adorno, who for Henrich comes off by far the worse in comparison to Heidegger (who is, rather, sheltered by Henrich), was certainly impertinent enough to transfer all-inclusively (and that means with less analytical expense than necessary) the accounts of such incommensurable moments to the credit of "aesthetic expansions of the autonomy of the modern subject."[6] According to Adorno, these expansions contain with all mourning "the normative force of a memory"—"anamnesis of repressed nature," as the parataxis essay phrases it.[7] This was directed against the likewise all-inclusive restitution of an 'aura,' which Adorno recognizes in Hölderlin as fallen into ruin, "drowned in mourning" as he says further on in the same essay. Heidegger's reading of the holiday hymn (*Wie wenn am Feiertage . . .*), on the other hand, had let Hölderlin's mourning persist in its withdrawal "into the thought of the One." "Remembrance of mourning"—as Heidegger unites the two concepts conclusively together—remains "near to that which has seized it and appears to be far. Mourning does not disappear in the departure of what has been simply lost. It lets the absent always return."[8]

Heidegger's interest is fixed on the fact that this return is grounded in the persistence of mourning, and for the sake of this return he fails to recognize the further deepening of mourning that occurs in the failure of the poem. He closes his eyes before definitive facts such as the one his dedication to the first of the *Erläuterungen*, the 1936 address "Hölderlin and the Essence of Poetry," calls to mind: "Norbert von Hellingrath/fallen on 14 December 1916 at Verdun/in memoriam." This dedication had not been reprinted before the text of the Gesamtausgabe (1982), where the now obsolete place is still missing: the subject now is no longer Verdun and also the original commentary, according to which the "publication" was justified "solely" by the dedication to Hellingrath, fallen at Verdun, was for the editor no longer fit for print.[9] We do not find ourselves under the Mediterranean light of Valéry's *Cimetière marin* in 1936, on the twentieth anniversary of Hellingrath's death, but on the fields of Verdun, and what counted most for Heidegger in Hölderlin—"in an outstanding sense the poet of poets," who sets everybody "in decision"— was "solely" the return of the fallen dead. Around the Verdun krypt circles Heidegger's thought that has made him a prisoner of the *Inability to Mourn*.[10] Henrich, for whom 'subjectivity' means that place to which all unity "as a last and imperishable ground" returns, underestimates Adorno's intuition: namely, to see the point of Hölderlin's poetry in its resistance to the idealist self-misunderstanding of the author.[11] Both Adorno and Heidegger, however, are taken by the impression of the insane poet, who for Adorno was 'beyond subjectivity' and, that is for Heidegger, "had long been taken into the protection of the night of madness."[12]

My argument unfolds in opposition to the constellation sketched above. I will first follow the "path of remembrance" that Henrich has proposed, in order to come to the "dark underside" of this "deceptively simple" poem.[13] Henrich's characterization has the advantage of a concise reconstruction, one suited to making this by no means simple poem, with all its underground darkness, surveyable at a single glance. I will then concentrate on the single sentence that, according to the opinion of numerous interpreters, contains the text's fascination, without letting more be derived from its grammatical placement than the immediate quality of its appeal whose charm produces an unexplained effect: *Im Hofe aber wächset ein Feigenbaum*—"But in the courtyard a figtree grows." In the succession of carefully prepared phrases, an observation made by interpreters before Henrich, this sentence stands in the secret middle that the figtree itself occupies. The "palpable presence," which Henrich, on the basis of the road to *Andenken*, finds in this middle, has its counterpart in that other sentence, entirely given to poetological reflection, at the end of the poem: the famous *Was bleibet aber, stiften die Dichter*—"But what remains, establish the poets." Between both foci of the poem, the popular gnome at the end and the romantically transfigured image at the beginning, Henrich's interpretation manufactures a connection whose fragility I now want to address.

Of course the relationship between intuition and reflection is too banal to be declared, without further notice, as the substance of the poem. In general, it constitutes a good portion of Hölderlin's ideological susceptibility, which promotes its suitability to philosophemes, so that his poems are interspersed with such quotable sentences as "But what remains, establish the poets." Only the equally parody-prone *Wo aber Gefahr ist, wächst das Rettende auch*—"Wherever is danger, there grows what saves" is more popular. Its popularity in the bourgeois discourses of cultural criticism has been parodied in a similarly blasphemous verse from Wilhelm Busch near the end of the nineteenth century: *Wer Sorgen hat, hat auch Likör*—"Who has cares, has liquor also".[14] In the case of the endowment of the poet, one finds the likewise odious point in Erich Fried: *Was bleibt, geht stiften*—"What remains, runs away." It is clear; what lends itself to parody here can be recognized as philosophically attractive even in the gestures of its denial.[15] Accordingly, a philosophically informed interpretation of Hölderlin has orientated itself around such gnomic enclaves in his texts, and his poetological interpretation cannot help but take for pure coin such sentences in which the intention of the author seems preeminently to pay off.

We have to contemplate here, if only for philological reasons, the genre to which these maxims belong, thus also those models in the Greek choral lyric, and above all Pindar, according to whose standard Hölderlin composed his poems. In this pre-philosophical lyric, whose greatness Hölderlin strove to equal, the key function of the gnome that later theoretical interpretation has found so congenial cannot be decisive for the substance of the poem. One can almost regard it as the essential point of the Hölderlinian undertaking that he sought, in deference to Pindar, an original unity of poetic intention, which preceded the later split caused by allegorical interpretation. This split became a fixed schema only in allegory. In this one point of Hölderlin's dealings with the Greeks, Heidegger's interpretations are congenial; it would be too circuitous to elucidate the individual details, but in this one respect Heidegger appears to me to correspond exactly to Hölderlin's poetic intention—more precisely than that intention corresponds to the contents of his own misguided interpretative strategies and results. On the other hand, interest in the origin of the concept of allegory seems to guide de Man's evaluation of Heidegger in the same way as it determines his reading of Hölderlin.

Heidegger himself was not aware of this poetological implication of his own readings, nor did he manage to keep allegorical interpretation at bay. Nevertheless, what has subsequently remained important for readings of *Andenken* in particular is what finally Wolfgang Binder has brought to the commonplace of the "realistic, unmythic" poem that *Andenken* is supposed to be, a poem whose dimensions are not mythic in the sense of disclosing themselves through an appropriate allegoresis of its contents.[16] In such an evaluation remains virulent—from Heidegger to Henrich—another interpretive intention, one which, in Dilthey's title *Das Erlebnis und die Dichtung*, of "lived experience and poetry," gets continuously funneled into its trivial consequences, though this already for Dilthey himself did not possess the banality that later one is accustomed to associate with it. Henrich does not subscribe to flat misunderstandings, for example the assertion that the object of *Andenken* is the actual experience of the poet in Bordeaux, but takes the concept of experience as the basis for the *act* of remembrance in Hölderlin.[17] I will neglect this part, which engages Fichte (Henrich speaks of *Aktuosität*), limiting myself to its consequences for the understanding of texts, and begin with a paraphrase of Henrich's results, as far as they are relevant to the figtree in the center of the poem.

Henrich's objective throughout is not to leave the "triad of key verses" to isolated speculations, the last of which is the oft-quoted commonplace about what remains in poetry, but rather to develop them along "the road to *Andenken*" as it unfolds in the poem. Thus he speaks of the architecture of the poem, which above all must be reconstructed before the concluding gnome as capstone of the whole edifice can be assessed. What, however, determines the road to remembrance before it comes to its gnomic poeticization are stations of *Vergegenwärtigung*, of 'making present' the landscape whose experience Hölderlin brought home with him as a 'souvenir' of his stay in Bordeaux. The bordelais landscape is visualized in two parts: in the first half the inner layout of the city; in the second half the outer contour of the land stretching to the sea. Henrich provides the historical topography in greater detail. It is not the case, however, as one could easily misunderstand him, that he seeks to explain the progress of the poem from a reality represented within it. What he intends, on the contrary, is to demonstrate landscape, as it appears in the poem, as a 'phenomenal' construction of remembrance. To be sure, the factual topography of Bordeaux is necessary for nothing but the identification and verification of the achieved constitution occuring in the poem. 'Landscape' as poetic construction—thus I read Henrich—is the object on which remembrance reflects the conditions of its constitution. This, in turn, permits explication in terms most suitable to the idealist idiom, and that means consistent with the historical intentionality of the author. Yet the poem *Andenken*, insofar as it is *Andenken*, cannot be subsumed under this intention.

In the first of the two constructions of landscape the northeasterly wind, with its accompanying inspiration motif, sets in—"The nor'easter blows"—and evokes, in the gesture of greeting admired by Heidegger, "The lovely Garonne/And the gardens of Bordeaux."[18] There, one finds the following image developed in deictic gestures evoked from memory:

> Dort, wo am scharfen Ufer
> Hingehet der Steg und in den Strom
> Tief fällt der Bach, darüber aber
> Hinschauet ein edel Paar
> Von Eichen und Silberpappeln;
>
> Noch denket das mir wohl und wie
> Die breiten Gipfel neiget
> Der Ulmwald, über die Mühl',
> Im Hofe aber wächset ein Feigenbaum.

> *There, where along the sharp cove*
> *Trails the path and into the river*
> *Deep dives the stream, but over it*
> *Looks out a noble pair*
> *Of oaks and silver poplars;*
>
> *It still comes back to me how*
> *The broad tops of the elm wood*
> *Bend over the mill,*
> *But in the courtyard a figtree grows.*

The 'precision' of representation (Henrich does not shy away from speaking about precision, yet substitutes the concept of representation with that of *Vergegenwärtigung*, of presentification or making present) begins "where along the sharp cove/Trails the path," a description that according to Henrich's determination meets the dominant formal features of the harbor of Bordeaux, the "port de la lune," which already in the Roman era was so named *portus lunae*. Its sharply cut bow is bordered by a narrow pier, which copies the shoreline lying adjacent to the city. Just as this pier, which brings the harbor into relief before the steeply fluctuating tidal shore, marks the constitution of the remembered image in the perspective of the city, so too are the following details of the picture arranged as markings of the same perspective: the stream emptying down into the ocean from the precipitous cliff; the pair of trees above on the same shore.[19] Its focal point, itself marked by the maintenance of the lyrical I at the beginning of the next stanza (*Noch denket das mir wohl . . .* —"It still comes back to me . . . "), lies in the gardens on the outskirts of Bordeaux, in a mill beneath elms in whose inner boundary appears before the outer-to-inner-turning gaze—the figtree.

I say appear, for that is the peculiar, questionable point in Henrich's depiction, the fact that "a still more life-like present" lights up in the self-reflexive turning of the perspective to a personal focal point, as if it could succeed in making present the landscape in the outline of its objects. And Henrich does not resist the attempt to regard the perception as 'symbolic,' heightened in reflection to its conditions of constitution, nor to elucidate allegorically, according to the standard measures of tradition, the figtree as such a perceptual symbol: The gaze (or rather the picture made present in it) "slides across into the inner court of the mill where the figtree grows. It must have appeared to the poet already at that time, as he saw it, as the middle point of a configuration of sense: the tree in front of the wall of Troy (in the hymn *Mnemosyne*) and by the grave of Semele (in the *Bacchae*-translation), the tree of paradise at the entrance to the history of human consciousness."[20]

The priority of an originary perception made present in the poem—one that seems to be carried forward in the poem ("already at that time, as he saw it"), for all its symbolic suitability ("as the middle point of a perceptual complex") and its secondary allegorical rationalization ("at the entrance to the history of human consciousness"—remains unquestioned and uncontested by Henrich. He strengthens, for all his disagreement with Heidegger's general tendency of imputation, the decisive point in Heidegger's interpretation, one which de Man derived from Heidegger's reading of the concluding gnome "But what remains, establish the poets." In de Man's comment—"what signifies for Heidegger: the poet founds the immediate presence of Being in naming it."[21] Henrich's description, one must of course add, gives to this understanding a precise poetic sense, one whose dimension Heidegger's intention transcends. As de Man's critique shows, one cannot accuse Hölderlin of any "nostalgia for the originary immediate" ("a state in which there is nothing, in sum, to say"); on the contrary, Hölderlin agrees with Hegel insofar as "it is not enough to have seen Being, for the difficulty only begins *after* this moment." What poets are able "to establish," then, cannot be "parousia": "for from the point that speech is uttered, it destroys the immediate and discovers that, instead of speaking Being, it can only speak mediation." Henrich's reconstruction of the originary perception reconstituted in the reflection of remembrance cannot but demonstrate this finding.

It is worth asking, then, what brings Henrich to elevating the figtree in the center of the poem ("there in the middle") to that "still more life-like present" cited above. It is, as I have indicated, the idealistic preoccupation with the reflection of reflection, which the subject fashions after itself. In Hölderlin's *Andenken*, however, this is not only thematic but also problematic. To be sure, the images that Henrich teaches us to see are most pregnant, but it is not the precision of the phenomenological reduction that is at stake here and whose potency in the description of landscape since the eighteenth century is well known. That Hölderlin brings before our eyes what Henrich later points out does not mean that he has done anything more than quoted the effects of this descriptive tradition. The effect of quotation, however, is that in the thematically constructed mode of experience, e.g., the mode of remembrance, it always thematizes something else along with the lived experience brought before our eyes, namely, the reflection that has superseded this experience. Henrich treats this reflection like a rhetorical ornament. But the primary

concern of the poem as poem is not the philosophical problematic of constitution that Henrich so skillfully reconstructs,
however much it might have been the concern of Hölderlin
the philosopher. If one takes Henrich's own demand seriously,
namely that the 'thinking of' within the poem can only be
"completed" *as* remembrance in the poem, then the relationship between the poem's own reflection and what is reflected
in the poem must be reversed. Remembrance would go from
being the vehicle of thinking, self-thematized in the poem, to
its tenor, while that which one is accustomed in the received
sense to regard as tenor would become vehicle and would find
itself reflected as vehicle.[22]

The figtree is in fact the insurpassable symbol in which
from time immemorial perspective has consolidated itself as
the 'symbolic form' of landscape and thus from which may be
read the displacement of allegorical self-interpretation.[23] John
Freccero has treated the decisive stage in the process of this
displacement, localizing it in Petrarch's poetics under the
title, appropriately enough, "The Figtree and the Laurel." I do
not want to go into the history of hidden Petrarchism
evinced in Hölderlin's poem, but Frecchero's juxtaposition of
figtree and laurel is highly instructive. One would of course
have to take other figtrees of Hölderlin into account. As far as
Andenken is concerned, new research has supplemented Henrich's observation to the effect that the "sharp coast" across
from Bordeaux, from which the poet's gaze turns to the interior courtyard, might refer to the laurel hill of Lormont (however pertinent we may also find the etymology of Lormont as
"hill of laurel").[24] Accordingly, what is important here is the
withdrawal of the poet's gaze from an implicit laurel to an explicit figtree—a silencing of poetic ambition that, in the concealment, appears not so much withdrawn but accentuated.
Which brings us back to Petrarch.

Petrarch carried out his relationship with Augustine in
the competition between laurel and figtree, and it is here
where we find what we need for Hölderlin's *Andenken*—the
courtyard in which it grows. In the *Confessions*, Augustine remembers the moment of his conversion *sub quadam fici ar-*

bore (VIII, 12, 28). In a preceding chapter of the same book, he mentions the courtyard where his conversion took place, *hortulus*, which could not be better translated into German than by Hölderlin's *Hof* where the figtree is found. It remains to be mentioned that in the same passage Augustine begins to talk of the powerful struggle of his "inner house," *interioris domus meae*, in whose "innermost chamber, his heart," the decision prepared the way, *in cubiculo nostro, corde meo* (VIII, 19). The parallelism of places is not incompatible with Henrich's reading, but when it comes to the turn of the gaze it becomes clear that we are not dealing with topology in the geographical sense. Rather, it is the old background metaphoric of memory whose rhetorical substrate both Augustine, in his rhetorical doctrine, as well as Hölderlin, who grew up in the late development of the same historical formation, effectively stage. The figtree was already for Augustine a quotation that had to do with conversion in the most precise sense, as well as with the difference between nature and culture in the widest sense, as the evangelists attest, and there in particular the most extremely effective rhetoric that Jesus employed to win his disciples (an example of which would be Nathanael in John 1: 48).[25] Augustine, like Hölderlin, was aware of the double tradition of the figtree in both Homer and the Bible, which he had come to distinguish as *umbra* and *figura*. Petrarch presupposes all this in the first book of his *Secretum* as he recalls the figtree and everything that occurred within its shadow in a fictive dialogue between his alter ego Francesco and his superego Augustine. Freccero gives a pregnant summary: "The figtree in the garden of Milan, . . . under the shade of which all this takes place, stands for a tradition of textual authority that extends backwards in time to the Logos and forward to the same Logos at time's ending, when both desire and words are finally fulfilled."[26]

A garden in Mailand, a courtyard in Bordeaux: both encapsulate the same mnemonic mark where the inward-turning gaze finds its orientation and the thinking of remembrance finds its haven. The testimony of Petrarch includes the fictive admonition of Augustine to hold the remembrance of the figtree higher in estimation than the poetic laurel; in other words, to take Augustine's book more seriously than his own songs to Laura, the *Canzoniere*. But what makes it important is the character of the mark that, beyond every distinction between poetry and truth, distinguishes the figtree before other signs of remembrance. For Petrarch lets there be no doubt that he is not deceived by Augustine's rhetoric that in the autobiographical fiction of the *Confessions* gives the figtree priority over the laurel. In this he precedes Hölderlin, and Hölderlin brings him to an end. In the end, both renounce the play of empty words—crowned by the laurel—as the pretext of poets, and thus both write to this end. The 'institution' accomplished by the poet (*Stiften*) lies in the—etymologically motivated—'stiffening' of signs (*Stiften/Versteifen*).[27] In this stiffening, what remains is guaranteed in the permanence of *Buchstaben*, the fixed letters, not in any constant or consistent meaning. What remains, so the figtree shows, is the signifier it is, and remains in the exchange of contexts. Irrespective of whether Augustine made up the figtree of his conversion or whether he owes it to some arbitrariness of circumstance, it is there for Hölderlin to find it again in the courtyard of a mill or in his own imagination.[28]

But the point of the concluding gnome is even more precise than Henrich's reading could have made it. "But what remains" remains in opposition ("but"); and this opposition is not only the one in which this last line is brought to what does not remain, namely that which is as unreliable as the "memory" of the sea, with its shifting tides, and the "eyes of love" fixed (*geheftet*) in desire—a Petrarchism par excellence. Previously, in the second landscape of the poem, turning the gaze to the sea, Hölderlin had been talking about the "painters" who refer back to the eighteenth-century thematics of *Ut pictura poesis*. There the constitution of landscape is analogous to the profits of maritime commerce: the seafolk ("men," "friends") whose farewell in the distance constitutes the perspective of this scene—"They/Like painters, bring together/ The beauty of the earth." Such fleeting compositions, as painters bring them before our eyes in the referential illusion of their representations, should be contrasted with the last verse: "But what remains, establish the poets." To this belongs, as a silent implication, that which the laurel hill of Lormont conceals: the fact, namely, that exactly there, on this hill, as Jean Pierre Lefebvre has argued, the painters and engravers of the time produced their views of Bordeaux. *Andenken* does not give us such a view (*Ansicht*); rather it exposes the construction of such a view. What, on the contrary, is established in this poem is the 'solid letter' (*der veste Buchstab*) that also in the poem *Patmos*, where Hölderlin uses these words, owes its existence to the instituting force of a poet (St. John "the Seer"). A comforting conclusion only if one wanted to underestimate the failure that is firmly maintained on the way of *Andenken* in the poem. The success of the figtree—far from any originary experience that could be 'made present,' but rather demanding a powerful tradition whose evocation comes from the illusionary effect of such fictive immediacy—is the success of the laurel. Because it is the laurel that still remains effective in the renunciation of empty ambition. This ambition's trace is contained in the concealment of the silenced desire. Momentary evidence, the motive for conversion, has left it behind.

Postscript[29]

Henrich insists on "grasping the poem as a whole," as he had on the occasion of a much younger tree, Apollinaire's *Arbre*.[30] To what extent does the parallelism of aesthetic experience and phenomenological reflection, which Henrich seems to presuppose in his analysis of the landscape in *Andenken* as the 'lived experience' of the poet (in the strict sense of Husserl), imply a concept of totality? Such a postulate would not have first been questioned in Apollinaire's *Arbre*, but it would have been put into question 'always already' in Hölderlin and Petrarch. The question then would be to what extent does the semiotic qualification of the figtree (as an 'indicated signifier' or 'interpretant' in Peirce's sense, as Paul Fry underscores) necessarily explode classical concepts of an organic whole of poetry, which have their ideal in the symbol? Indeed. Or, more precisely, to what extent is this failed totality the postulate of a philosophical aesthetics that finds nothing in art but the poor imitation of its ideal? Thus Reinhart Herzog refers me to the fact that probably one of the models that the tradition had in stock for Augustine's figtree was the plane-tree of Plato's *Phaedrus* (230a–e). The irony already present in Plato is a presupposition of the hidden quotation in Augustine.[31] In the transformation of the plane-tree into the figtree, one could say, pure appearance (*aisthesis*) appears to be deprived of its *nonconstructedness*—a rhetoric of evidence which is part of conversion, as of every *conversio* in this tradition.

To quote a distinction Wolfgang Iser has used with respect to Hölderlin: "In the selectivity of schemata ['landscape'] it [the subject constituted in 'remembrance'] achieves its individual precision"; but equally so, and this is decisive, "in the selectivity of relationships of schemata to each other it achieves its historical precision."[32] This means that the historical pertinence of the figtree undermines in the act of remembrance (as the 'thinking of' of the poem, as Henrich puts it), the identity and unity of *Andenken* as a poem. Indeed, what is at stake in this poem is not just a heightened interest in the object "for the sake of its appearance," as one could quote Husserl.[33] Rather, what makes the figtree a symbol, in the most general sense, is the totalizing force it has had for cultural anthropology when it came to the apostrophied difference between nature and culture.[34] Certainly: it "grows" in Hölderlin's line and this growing is the name—stylized by Rilke in the first of the *Sonnets to Orpheus*—for the organic formation of the symbol (sixteenth *Duino Elegies*). At the same time, the historical index of this naming includes the symbolic markedness of the sign, which turns the figtree into what it is as 'quoted' and wants to be as 'experienced live.' Because it is precisely the cultural manipulation of the natural growth of the fig, which makes the figtree in the bible into the salvific symbol: the lance wound, which confirms the death of Christ on the cross, is still to be read according to this model.[35]

What prefigures the puncture of the lance is the perforation of the fruit with a specially curved instrument, the 'caprification,' as a result of which insects trigger fructification. (Compared to this, the medical pseudo-explanations of St. John's testament prove to be pointless.)

It is thus not by coincidence that St. John makes this symbol the most efficient of Jesus' devices, and grounds it in the artificial redemption of the maturation process of the fig. Already John's treatment of Nathanael's conversion (1:50) bears the marks of near-ironic self-reflection on the rhetorical means employed. Augustine's *Confessions* restage the rhetorical evidence that had been established in John. Petrarch's *Secretum* gives away the secret of this staging and exposes it as a rhetorical operation. The historicity of the motive in Hölderlin reflects, then, the rhetoricity of the means employed. He enforces the stability of the figure established by St. John the poet through the variation of contexts—including his own. This has devastating consequences for the affected contexts—including his own—though different ones in the historically different configurations of Augustine, Petrarch, or Hölderlin. In Augustine's *conversio* the figtree signifies a turning point, which in Petrarch's reading becomes visible as a benchmark for poetic convertibility (*tropus*). It disappears in Hölderlin with the completion of this turning, in which it has become translucent. The figtree is a laurel but a displaced one—the true palm, if one followed Klopstock's optimistic reading of Young's "Let not the Laurel, but the Palm, inspire!" As renounced ambition and secret desire it remains—"but"—still effective in the text, which it discredits, and still bears witness—"but"—to the efficacy of a discourse, which—fallen into discredit—nevertheless goes on—a discourse cancelled and crossed out.[36] This restriction may be one of the implications of that which Heidegger—also with regard to this "but"—had in mind when he spoke about "the joint [*Fuge*] of the but [*aber*]," which is for him the whole poem: *eine einzige in sich gefügte Fuge des aber*.[37] In its entirety, however, deeply divided.

The secrecy of the laurel, to quote Rilke once more (*selbst in der Verschweigung*), is the perspective of this divide, implicit counterpoint, which Rilke's *Sonnets to Orpheus* broach from the first stanzas on, yet also let disappear in the configurations of the sonnets (in the "song"). Reading Hölderlin resembles to a large extent a reading of Rilke, which transcends this circumstance and instead holds to the suggestively maintained ("sung") objects ("things"), without being aware of their sign-character in the reading or even wanting to admit it.[38] Rilke's Petrarchism designates only what has been implicit in the tradition of 'motive' since Petrarch himself.[39] A look into the palimpsest-like substratum of his otherwise 'modern' landscape demonstrates this *in extenso*.[40] In his landscape trees are 'bookmarks' in a precise sense; they resemble Lacan's 'upholstery buttons' insofar as they fix the patchwork of the text to the hermeneutical framework of tradition, *mutatis mutandis* guide the eye through the arrangement of representations.

The 'isotopy' of trees in Hölderlin's *Andenken* thus implicates the Lorbeer of Lormont: from their first paired appearance ("a noble pair/Of oaks and silver poplars") to their denuded condition ("beneath/The denuded mast") all the possibilities are represented. Already in Petrarch's *Canzoniere* the disappearance of the laurel *in* the landscape, its quiet presence in the natural surroundings of trees, is a characteristic of landscape experience. Yet in Hölderlin's *Andenken* this latency, with which Petrarch maintains the play of his words, goes deeper. It is no longer to be brought to momentary appearance. What remains for him is a pattern discarded for all time but still active in latency, a paradigm that at once motivates and threatens, vacillates in the ambivalence of its Augustinian investment without being able to escape from the *Fort* again into the *Da* of Petrarchan, narcissistic play (*Fort/da*). What constitutes Petrarchism—widely unrecognized, concealed in its linguistic work on myth—is not only the oxymoronic joint, as Forster insists, but its poetic deepening.[41] What endures in the joint ("but"), historically developed, structurally remaining, is named *Stiften*, *Andenken*, not "Laura" (like the laurel) and "Diotima" (the Greek woman). *Andenken* thinks its thinking of as the impossibility of its, of every remembrance and leaves behind in its trace the figure excluded, a sign of this, of every remembrance. It thinks structure as the impossibility of that which it inaugurates. In the poem *Mnemosyne*, the death of Mnemosyne, of enabling memory (the mother of the muses) is this impossible structure's most intimate and final conclusion. There we hear about a traveler, who goes "talking of the cross," "From far intimating/The other": with Achilles, "By the figtree . . . dead."

IV. Wild Elder—The Churchyard
(Hölderlin and Kant)

Der Kirchhof

Du stiller Ort, der grünt mit jungem Grase,
Da liegen Mann und Frau, und Kreuze stehn,
Wohin hinaus geleitet Freunde gehn,
Wo Fenster sind glänzend mit hellem Glase.

Wenn glänzt an dir des Himmels hohe Leuchte
Des Mittags, wann der Frühling dort oft weilt,
Wenn geistige Wolke dort, die graue, feuchte
Wenn sanft der Tag vorbei mit Schönheit eilt!

Wie still ist's nicht an jener grauen Mauer,
Wo drüber her ein Baum mit Früchten hängt;
Mit schwarzen thauigen, und Laub voll Trauer,
Die Früchte aber sind sehr schön gedrängt.

Dort in der Kirch' ist eine dunkle Stille
Und der Altar ist auch in dieser Nacht geringe,
Noch sind darin einige schöne Dinge,
Im Sommer aber singt auf Feldern manche Grille.

Wenn Einer dort Reden des Pfarrherrn hört,
Indeß die Schaar der Freunde steht daneben,
Die mit dem Todten sind, welch eignes Leben
Und welcher Geist, und fromm seyn ungestört.

The Churchyard

You quiet place that greens with young grass,
There lie husband and wife, and crosses stand,
Where, on their way out, friends go
Where windows are shining with clear glass.

When shines on you the sky's high lamp
Of midday, when spring there often lingers,
When spiritual cloud there, the grey, the moist
When softly the day with beauty hastens!

How quiet is it not on that grey wall,
Where yonder a tree hangs with fruit;
With black dewy ones, and leaves of mourning,
The fruit, however, is very beautifully clustered.

There in the church is a dark quiet
And also the altar is in this night dim,
Still inside there are some fine things,
In summer many a cricket in the fields sing.

When One hears there the clergyman's talk,
While the band of friends stand beside,
Who are with the dead, what a life of one's own
And what spirit, and being pious, undisturbed.

[Chadwick's translation]

Instead of an epigraph: "I am now orthodox,
Your Holiness! No, no! I am studying
the third volume of Mr. Kant and am very
busy with the new philosophy."[1]

Kant, in the introduction to his essay *On Eternal Peace*
of 1795, comes unexpectedly to speak about the double sense
of his title, a word play that at first glance one would not
have expected and which he immediately wants to satirize. On
the first page of the original edition, after repeating the title
and distancing it with a clear stroke, he writes the following
commentary:

> Whether this satirical title from a Dutch innkeeper's
> shield, on which a churchyard was painted, represents hu-
> manity in general or, in particular, the heads of state who
> can never get enough of war, or perhaps even only the
> philosophers who dream those sweet dreams—it is open
> to discussion.[2]

To compare the title of a book with the name of a restaurant
means to take metonomy at its name, that is, the preposition
zum, which names in one instance the 'contents' and in the
other, 'place.' To equate the determination of place with that
of contents (the classical instance of the transference of names
that is metonomy) can depend in the present case on an equiv-
ocation of the German *zum*, whose ambiguity Kant must have
suddenly become aware of (Latin *de* in one case, *ad* or *apud* in
the other).

Kant does not want to get mixed up with the euphemism
of the inn's sign, which uses the blessing connected with the
establishment's name both as an invitation and—according to
its location and character—as an advertisement. This euphemism can't be better discredited than with a tavern whose
location next to a cemetary has spurred the innkeeper on to
the promising expression of 'eternal peace'—a felicitous mix-

ture of conviviality and marketing savvy for which Holland is well known as its most satirical topos. The joke, which Kant derives from these acts of naming, is, however, all the better when he passes off taverns in general and Dutch ones in particular as the appropriate genre of the fool's paradise, as the reverse side of that otherworldly hope for paradise from which Kant's 'philosophical design' seeks to secure a reasonable side—'eternal peace' as the only reasonable utopia.[3]

The Dutch innkeeper, one could say, has been around the block a time or two and therefore never misses an opportunity for a pun, such as when he illustrates the name of his establishment "At the Eternal Peace" (*Zum ewigen Frieden*) with the picture of a "cemetery" (*Friedhof*). Averse to base cynicism of this kind, even if apparently not unimpressed by it, Kant turns to the concoction of satirical remedies. The threefold allegorical reading to which he submits the innkeeper's sign derives the moral of the story (in the manner of a *subscriptio*) from the relationship of the *inscriptio* "At the Eternal Peace" to the *pictura* of the churchyard, a moral indeed that goes against the grain of the allegorical intention of the art of emblems. The collapse of anagogy diagnosed by Benjamin, the futility of every 'post-figural construction,' as some have tried to put a better face on it, could not be more satirically employed than in Kant's words.[4] *Allegorically*, this emblem pronounces the mortality of "humanity in general"; *tropologically*, the necrophilia of enlightened heads of state (more than the melancholy of baroque monarchs) "who never can get enough of war"; *anagogically*, the aloofness and naïveté of philosophers "who dream those sweet dreams." A tavern that promises eternal peace—and a peace thanks to those "who *never get enough* of war"—flagrantly renders all morality and anagogy superfluous; to go there replaces, for those who feel at home in such a place, any morality and anagogy. In the collapse of both allegorical perspectives, which the sign of the Dutch innkeeper valorizes to a slogan of business, can be read "the rule of reflection," as Kant elsewhere has shown in the *Critique of Judgement*, in the venerable example of a *Handmühle* (the famous handgrinder of section 59), according to which the allegorical reflection in this emblem functions or, in this case, doesn't function—and that is the satire.[5]

According to a suggestion by Sattler, Hölderlin used Kant's Dutch innkeeper's sign in one of his later poems, which under the title *Das fröhliche Leben* (*The Happy Life*) employs a good number of other practical jokes, along with a whole series of orthodox sources of bourgeois ideology, in particular that great standard, Schiller's ode *To Joy*, in whose poetic meter *The Happy Life* was composed so that it could be sung to Beethoven's melody.[6] Nor is the Hegelian dialectic missing in Hölderlin's poem, a dialectic in opposition to which Sattler, as well as the whole body of Hölderlin researchers, wants to restore everything in Hölderlin that has been revoked since Hegel. Sattler's hunch was paralleled in Adorno's *Negative Dialectics*, which brings Kant's 'eternal peace' together with "Beethoven's composition of the Kantian hymn to joy." Adorno is concerned with the musical accent on "must," which Beethoven "in the spirit of Kant" introduces into Schiller's text, a text which Adorno himself, apparently in the same Kantian spirit, falsely recites: *Muß ein ewiger* [instead of *lieber*] *Vater wohnen*—"An eternal [instead of "dear"] father must dwell."[7] The mistake is not without a hidden point; the postponement of the love of the father to such a questionable eternity makes this forced transcendence, at which Adorno takes affront, all the more crass. Adorno is persuaded by a consonance with Kant's eternal peace that does not resonate in Schiller's excessive pathos. Adorno did not think of Hölderlin, whose late parodic talent must have been equally foreign to him (just as the same Hölderlin's resistance to Schiller's affirmative pathos would have been congenial). Mindful of the "starry heavens over us" in Kant's introduction of the categorical imperative, Adorno stresses the transcendental borders that Schiller's joy strives to overcome: "Brothers—over the starry heavens," reads the *Ode to Joy*. According to Adorno, Kant in the end came to discard all "metaphysical ideas, in particular the idea of immortality, caught in the representations of space and time and thus limited to them." Thus Kant is said by Adorno to have "scorned the transition to affirmation" that

Schiller overplays in his ode. *The Happy Life* of Hölderlin (second stanza) quotes the innkeeper's shield as follows:

> O vor diesem sanften Bilde,
> Wo die grünen Bäume stehn,
> Wie vor einer Schenke Schilde
> Kann ich kaum vorübergehn.

> *Oh before this pleasant picture*
> *Where the green trees grow*
> *As before a tavern's shield*
> *I can't resist to go.*

Hölderlin here perfectly lives up to Kant's satirical intention. Not that he follows this intention, but rather reduces it to absurdity together with that against which this intention is directed. What remains is a picture, which rhymes with the sign (*Bilde* with *Schilde*), where Kant takes his departure and Hölderlin can hardly resist a pint. He speaks of the "pleasant picture" that is evoked by the annunciation of eternal peace (on the shield *Zum ewigen Frieden*), and he uses the same word for the pleasure of this picture as is used in Schiller's song:

> Alle Menschen werden Brüder
> Wo dein sanfter Flügel weilt . . .

That is, "Where your soft wings abide" (*sanfter Flügel* as in *sanftes Bild*). Hölderlin doesn't mention yet the contents of this picture, Kant's churchyard, which enters the poem several stanzas later. There it is precisely peace that is induced through the contemplation of this picture. The reason why staying in this picture is so irresistible stems from its contemplative character, whose softness is peace:

> Und Betrachtung giebt dem Herzen
> Frieden, wie das Bild auch ist,
> Und Beruhigung den Schmerzen,
> Welche reimt Verstand und List.

And contemplation induces in the heart
Peace, as this picture also is,
And lessening of pain,
Rhyming understanding with cunning.

There is no mention of the churchyard so far and there won't be any in this poem. But what is mentioned is the "lessening of pain," the *lesmosyne* that is caused by the contemplation of the picture, which is peace. The rhyme on "understanding and cunning"—Kantian and Hegelian terminology as in the limits of understanding and the cunning of reason (*List der Vernunft*)—ascribes as a remedy for the heart the alleviation of pain as a promise of peace and before it comes to it. A readiness for peace (*Friedfertigkeit*) is the quintessence of *Blödigkeit* and *Einfalt* (literally "stupidity" and "simplicity"). The emblem, whose satire Kant challenges, is taken by this peacefulness in its literalness, and that means: denuded of its allegorical multiplicity.[8]

Enlarged from the parodic manifesto that *The Happy Life* is, *The Churchyard*, apparently composed at the same time, presents itself as the "picture" of eternal peace, which invites good abode and promises "lessening of pain." Softness is the quality of this picture as of all the pictures around which Hölderlin's late poetry evolves. The image of peace that the churchyard (literally *Friedhof*) offers is the very idea of this gentle picturesque: *Ruhe sanft* (the equivalent of "rest in peace"). The peace and quiet of the cemetary—which for Kant depicts the most unwarranted of expectations because it takes the outcome of war (death) as the condition of the only possible peace—is elevated by Hölderlin, not without conscious comedy, to the condition of someone who is beyond laughter but has found his peace.[9] It is a peace "of the tame and of the pious" who "As from thorns uninjured" enters into happy life (first stanza). It is found, this peace, in the piety whose stupidity, *Blödigkeit*, had previously been in Hölderlin's earlier work the distinguishing mark of the poet's courage, *Dichtermut*. The biblical commonplace for Hölderlin's two poems entitled *Blödigkeit* and *Dichtermut* is to be found in Erasmus's

In Praise of Folly and whose quintessence is finally formulated in the half-sentence with which the *Kirchhof* poem breaks off: "and being pious, undisturbed."

Walter Benjamin has demonstrated how in the two early poems, *Dichtermut* and *Blödigkeit*, poet's courage and stupidity are the first conditions of "that inner life" that rhymes on joy and overcomes the "dissonance between image and life."[10] Reworking *Dichtermut* in *Blödigkeit*, Hölderlin rhymes *Sei zur Freude gereimt*, which means "Be rhymed for the fun of it," but which also means "Be converted to the joy of it." Eugen Gottlob Winkler, who first took the late Hölderlin's achievement as a poet seriously, correctly places the emphasis on the "renunciation" that makes the extended *simplicity* of the pictures "ungraspable" in their impenetrability.[11] The peaceful Erasmus aimed his work *In Praise of Folly*, when it came to a discussion of "sticks and stones" and everything else that could be quoted within the realm of "the lilies of the field," against the allegorical "assininities" of a Nikolaus of Lyra and took side instead with the stupidity of "his" Dutchmen, whose easy-going nature stood quite remote from academic subtleties. (With sophistries of this kind Erasmus later plied his trade at the three-language college in Leuven.)[12]

Sattler, when he found such serene comic effects in the later work of Hölderlin, thought they represented a regression: a "complete reversal" or "cathartic movement," in which *The Happy Life* produces "apparently harmless pictures drenched with obvious irony," "seemingly exoteric pictures, in truth concretized reflection." We have to evaluate this regression carefully, and this means with respect to Hölderlin's previous progress, which in his earlier work was always already in jeopardy and thus difficult to round off to the belated systematics offered by Hölderlin studies and the demands they make for the sake of their poet. If we take regression thus as repetition, remembrance, and working-through of the previous works, then we come to a different conclusion. The irony found by Sattler in the late work as an "ironically anticipatory repetition of the 'adolescent' Tübingen hymns," or even the accomplishment of a 'second childhood,' shows less of a regressive movement than a poetic momentum. It consists less in taking back old impulses than in maintaining an absolute distance from them.

The crux here lies not the least in what Hölderlin's last lyric represents for philological interpretation, namely, the exemplarity of late Hölderlin for the methodological embarrassment of literary hermeneutics since Schleiermacher's time. For in this lyric, poetics becomes indistinguishable from the relational frameworks of the psychology of 'lived experience' (Dilthey having been responsible for definitively grounding poetics in such psychologies). In other words, here, as undeniably nowhere else, the same, biologically identical author writes, from the moment of his 'madness,' texts that, on the one hand, can no longer be understood in continuity with his previous products and, on the other hand, cannot be read independently of those same texts. The disintegrating identity of the author Hölderlin only permits the symptoms of this disintegration to be recognized and, accordingly, perceived as nothing but documents of ruin. The tendency of research to find announced, thematized, or in any case comprehensible the moment of this plunge into lunacy, of this "schizophrenic disintegration" (Stierlin) in certain last poems before the madness (such as *Hälfte des Lebens*, as the convenient title seems to imply from Dilthey to Jaspers), this reading of the so-called *Spätwerk* has turned the last work into mere documents out of which speaks only undisguised illness. Whether the schizophrenic regression could be the only content of these last poems, or whether in them out of their predicament a relative virtue could still be ascertained (though of course not that which saves, from the famous line of *Patmos*—"Wherever is danger, there grows what saves"): whatever we think along these lines, the poetic achievement of the elderly Hölderlin draws its readability solely from the prognosis of illness. This achievement's poetic character would be completely defined by its restrictions. The superhuman effort of the last great poetic designs, so runs the devastating conclusion, appears to be reduced to the measure of human failure.

Even Szondi (to cite the most sensible judgment), when he shrewdly observed the "artificial, overextended distance that

Hölderlin was determined to create vis-à-vis the outside world as well as with himself and his poetry," cannot help but explain, elucidate, and understand all this with concepts like "derangement," "benightedness," and a final failing of "powers."[13] The "other arrow" Szondi discovered in Hölderlin is "interpreted as private suffering that goes astray in the objective task of the text."[14] Textual analyses flow very subtly into symptomatological assertions: faulty deixis and "introversive semiosis" (Jakobson), prevailing present tense and impoverished perception (Böschenstein), so runs the diagnosis into which, with a certain inevitability, linguistic and literary analysis gets transformed.[15] The rules of this convertibility are presupposed in the critical paradigm of *Erlebnis und Dichtung*, "lived experience and poetry," which in the case of 'poor Hölderlin' encounter their limits, the limits of a 'realism of experience' whose organ poetry was supposed to be.[16] Minimally, we would have to admit that a connection between poetry and experience is not to be denied, yet it lies not in the field of literary studies. Even if we do not want to make this connection completely abstract (because it belongs to the heuristic fiction of literary hermeneutics), we must be aware of the ruling modes of such misunderstanding. And even purely structural models can't afford to lose touch with the hermeneutical frames of understanding. But what, in the case of 'poor Hölderlin,' makes the poverty of the author into the embarrassment of a reading public is the impossibility of reading further than the knowledge of his illness reaches, to remain stuck with that which offers itself touchingly to one's own empathy. Whether he was a disguised Jacobin or a cloistered hermit doesn't make much difference; the advanced work of mourning that Pierre Bertaux wants to certify for Hölderlin can only superficially answer the question how "it was possible that a 37-year-old man could endure this vegetative existence for another 35 years"?[17]

Bertaux's, like Sattler's, insistence on the logic as well as the obstinacy of Hölderlin's withdrawal, the stoical as well as ironical moment of his reserve—all this has the advantage of not viewing the poetological questions incited by the late poems as already decided by the psychiatric framework of their creation. To take Hölderlin's alienation poetically and not

immediately to read the 'existential' moment of schizophrenic
withdrawal in the admittedly ironic movement of disengage-
ment—this means first and above all resisting hermeneutical
investigation, codes that decode, cryptics that unriddle, hidden things that explain: "Scardanelli," for example, his se-
mantics, his origin, his secret identity. For what falls entirely
out of view with this activity—misled by a semantic surface
of enormous simplicity—is the poetic constitution of the apparently simple, simplistically rhymed material in which people tend to find either the hidden intention of a stubborn
author or deep-seated symptoms of his madness—the "motive
of keeping things secret," for example, and its linguistic strategies.[18] What, on the contrary, becomes very obvious through
Sattler's research, in spite of the smooth rhymes of something
apparently confused, is not to be found in the depths over
which delusion broods, but in the unexpected proximity to old
motives that remain imperceptibly present in the new poems.
In such unbridgeable distance, as it offers itself, reigns a
unique introverted intertextuality in which the last poems return to the first: less "deep-coded," as Sattler would have it,
than deep-cogitated, as above all he has discovered.

Without being able to go into a detailed analysis of the
possible models of re-reading, usually dependent on develop-
mental concepts like progression and regression that set the
standard for the production of a lyrical oeuvre, in the break between Hölderlin's last poems and his previous work, including
the so-called late work, a radical condition can be found that
elsewhere is subordinated unconditionally to the hermeneutical demand for the harmony of 'lived experience' and poetry—
yet here the way is blocked. This blockage is nowhere more
conspicuous than in the exchange of names, the explicit repudiation of Hölderlin's name that corresponds to this repudiation (of 'foreclosure'), which 'the Name of the Father,'
according to Lacan and Laplanche, signifies for Hölderlin's
psychosis.[19] What the new names (Scardanelli above all) en-
code has, possibly, no other deeper meaning than the distancing from the father's name. As Sattler's commentary indicates,
this stands at the center of the poem The Churchyard, which

we have only in a transcript from his mother's hand and thus cannot compare with his own manuscript: "*The Churchyard is from the hand of my blessed mother, I wish therefore that she should again possess it,*" wrote Hölderlin's half-brother Karl Gock to Chr. Th. Schwab, who selected the poem in his Hölderlin collection of 1846.[20]

This *Churchyard*, like every churchyard, is not any arbitrary allegory, but rather the Christian allegory of allegory, an allegory of Christian interpretation and model from which the very idea of Christian interpretation of allegory can be read off. To be sure, there is nothing (decidedly nothing) to be observed here of the "comfortless confusion of Golgotha," which exacts, in Benjamin's characterization, transcendence as "allegory of resurrection."[21] Hölderlin literally 'sublates,' cancels and preserves at the same time, the hope, which was deprived of all prospects in the cynicism of the Dutch innkeeper, and was to be restored in Kant's practical reason. It is preserved in the 'view' that his late poems altogether offer; thus the frequent title among his late poems: *Aussicht*. Paradigmatically and literally, the view framed by Hölderlin's window is the conspicuous expression for the poetic "composedness" of the "pleasant pictures" that frame it, one picture of which is here quoted from its foreign, Kantian context, expounded and discarded. If *The Happy Life*, in its retreat from the world, alludes to the parable of parables (the one of the "sower" from *Patmos*) and, "Like from thorns uninjured," brings into play the fatal thorns of Mark 4: 3–9 (which are not mentioned in *Patmos*), then *The Churchyard* concerns the other end of the picture evoked there (which is dealt with in *Patmos* in a different way): namely, the *picture of harvest*.[22] In the allegory of *The Churchyard*, the "solid letter" and "German song" (*vester Buchstab* and *deutscher Gesang*), with whose care *Patmos* ends, are replaced by the "doctrine" of the "simile" and its interpretation, implicit in the parable of the sower and subsequently explicated by Jesus. It motivates an image that leaves aside the faith of the Gospel—of the "clergyman's talk" at the graveside. Instead, the formerly lyrical I makes its appearance in the last stanza as "One" who enjoys "a life of one's own" and, exempt from all last rites, thinks only of "spirit" and "being pious, undisturbed."[23]

The first stanza of The Churchyard is connected with the last through the farewell of friends, always renewed, from which the middle stanzas diverge into a perception that has long taken leave and leads for itself a "life of its own," while the continuous leave-taking of friends is apprehended together with the stillness of the place. There the greenness of the grass indicates the freshness of graves and the shining of the windows the position of the sun. A "life of one's own" survives in the regularity of year and day, on the margins of the life that is guided by the church and ultimately brought to rest in the cemetary. The place of this life is the peace and quiet of this churchyard. It is not the noise of clerical business:

> Wenn Einer dort Reden des Pfarrherrn hört,
> Indeß die Schaar der Freunde steht daneben,
> Die mit dem Todten sind, welch eignes Leben
> Und welcher Geist, und fromm seyn ungestört.

> When One hears there the clergyman's talk,
> While the band of friends stand beside,
> Who are with the dead, what a life of one's own
> And what spirit, and being pious, undisturbed.

The caesura occurs in the next to the last line; one would like to add a dash before the exclamation, "what a life of one's own," which sets itself off from the previous stanzas and frames them. It is highly doubtful that Hölderlin's mother was aware of her son's separation from the office of the church commemorated in this poem and secured in a picture she may have found persuasive, thus motivating her to copy the poem for her own meditation (perhaps to be placed in her prayer book). The turn to a life of his own is irrefutable. The "spirit" that accompanies the undisturbed piety is directed towards the picture of "eternal peace" that offers itself to contemplation. This spirit is touched from afar with the inspiration of the Göttin Freude addressed by Hagedorn and Klopstock (and quoted before Schiller from Shaftesbury) as the embodiment of ancient enthusiasm.[24]

However, the picture inscribed within this allegory of allegory, the picture of eternal peace, is not the promise of the afterlife that one comes to hear, no doubt, in the sermons of a clergyman; rather, it shows the promise of *this* life whose harvest, autumn, as completion of spring and summer, brings the allegory of the churchyard to fulfillment:

> Wie still ist's nicht an jener grauen Mauer,
> Wo drüber her ein Baum mit Früchten hängt;
> Mit schwarzen thauigen, und Laub voll Trauer,
> Die Früchte aber sind sehr schön gedrängt.

> *How quiet is it not on that grey wall,*
> *Where yonder a tree hangs with fruit;*
> *With black dewy ones, and leaves of mourning,*
> *The fruit, however, is very beautifully clustered.*

The quiet place, addressed in the manner of the classical ode, finds here, in the middle of the poem, its still center, apart from the performance of church functions. It is probably one of the most finished stanzas of Hölderlin's poetry, in which the "tree with fruit," as full of literary allusions as it is full of leaves of mourning, is mindful of another poem, *Half of Life*, where "With its yellow pears/And wild roses everywhere/The shore hangs in the lake," and, further down in the second half, "Walls stand cold and speechless." Over the churchyard walls there hangs another tree with its fruit—black, not colorful like the pear—in which the poem's dominant tone is sharpened from *Mauer*, wall, to *Trauer*, mourning: *grau, thauig, Laub*: gray, dewy, leaves.

It was again Sattler who identified the tree and fruit occupying the middle of the poem, secluded but magnificent, as the *Holunder* tree, the elder, death tree "of old," and the name of father Hölderlin—the elder from the father's garden and family coat of arms.[25] In the earlier ode *An Thills Grab* (At Thill's Grave), to which Sattler sees Hölderlin returning, the elder tree stands on a Schwabian poet's grave that Hölderlin had visited with Neuffer in 1789: "Ye quiet shadows of his elder tree soothe you," he addresses first the shadows and then the deceased precursor poet whom he never met: "Oh rest well, rest well, good man! you sleep so *softly*," goes the address *At Thill's Grave*, "in the quiet shade of your elder tree."[26] The address to the shadows of the tree, not to be confused with the shadows it casts over the grave of the poet, is performed in flight, in escape: "Hide me," he says to the tree, "that no one mock my tears and laugh . . . " The heavily concealed tears, hard to suppress in the presence of the elder, are not addressed to the one who rests in its shadows, although they dry "clinging to your mound" (fifth stanza). But this is not all that the name, handed down in arms and crests, brings to the surface. Already the first stanzas of the same poem treat of nothing other than that which in this place, before all poetic elevation and enhancement, returns from repression—the loss of the father—suffered before all remembrance. One could say that the pattern of the ode, localized "at" *Thill's Grave*, is actualized at this grave. The double sense of the preposition of its address is reassigned to the drama of the gifted child emerging in its shadows, shadows of poetic conversation with the precursor, and again finds at his grave, in the shadows "of its elder," the scene of this drama—a metonymic reduction like Kant's on the occasion of eternal peace.

What breaks forth at Thill's grave is a "series of corpses" (*Leichenreihen*) and even more pathetic his mother "deprived of her soul" (*entseelt*) at the death of his father, who, in the course of the poem, is remembered in the presence of Thill with the lyrical apostrophe: "Oh father! dear blessed one!" Johann Jakob Thill, lest we forget, died in the same year as Heinrich Friedrich Hölderlin; in other words, his tombstone bore the same death date as that of his father: 1772. What remains unclear in the dubious light of the relevant facts is the reference to which father, whether to this (Hölderlin's own) father or, as in the poem about *Die Meinigen* (*Those of Mine*), to his second father whose death he more consciously experienced. Hölderlin was two years old at the death of his father and nine at the death of his stepfather.[27]

Die Meinigen, one of the poet's earliest, urgently seeks reconciliation with his new family, which is his and yet does not carry his name, but, like his mother, carries the name of the second, thoroughly loved yet lost father; it maintains in tones of great distress the place among those whom he tirelessly contemplates as his family (*die Seinigen*). At the beginning, the poem remembers the founding hour of this troubled togetherness: "as once in our quiet hut,/Terrible! down your death angel came" (stanzas four and five). The "dreadful" object of address is here different than at Thill's grave. The earlier poem invokes "Master of worlds!" (first line), the name of the eternal father *in* the name of which—"In the name of the father"—the lost one, as "Eternally true father!," is proclaimed (stanza four). His mother, whose remembrance in the later poem is given first place—"And you, dear, good mother!" (third line)—is here not yet the object of address, though the object of longing: first she is the image of "woe," then, "imploring, sobbing," the image of "desire" (stanza five).

The first scene in *Die Meinigen* was too "pathetic" for Laplanche, who also missed its resumption in *At Thill's Grave.* He quotes Hölderlin's decisive, later letter to his mother of 18 June 1799, whose pointedness and insight leaves nothing to be desired. Hölderlin confronts his mother's *tristesse,* hardened in the unyielding devoutness of a merciless pietism, "a mourning endured by the *Widow Gok* with obstinacy and not without secret satisfaction," as Laplanche explains.[28] Likewise obstinately, Hölderlin offers his own origin of his "tendency to mourn," which in its own obstinacy is significant because it concerns the same cause, yet with reversed shares in its mechanism:

Also you, dear mother! have not given me this tendency to mourn, of which I cannot excuse myself completely. I see pretty clearly over my entire life, almost back to my earliest youth, and well know the time since my heart has tended in that direction. You will hardly believe me, but I still remember all too well. When my second father died, whose love was so unforgettable to me, when, with an incomprehensible pain, I felt like an orphan, and saw your daily mourning and tears, then my soul was attuned for the first time to this seriousness that never entirely left me and admittedly could only grow with the years.[29]

Not doubting the "truthfulness" of the passage, Laplanche in the end sees the truth preeminently in Hölderlin's "identification" with his mother, from whom, however, at least with respect to the explanation above, he does *not* want to derive his "tendency to mourn." Certainly, as Laplanche observes: "He connects his mourning inseparably with the mourning of his mother through an identification from which he explains he has not freed himself."[30] But Hölderlin's pain has become "incomprehensible" only because he connects its urgency inseparably with the "mourning and tears" of his mother instead of linking it to the "unforgettability" of his "dear father." Understandably, he felt "like an orphan," yet it is fully incomprehensible for him (and therefore his "tendency to mourn" is melancholic, aptly translated by Laplanche as "penchant à la tristesse") that the mourning that he ventures to assert as his own comes as a melancholy wholly alien to him, indebted to his mother's "daily mourning and tears." He sees himself overwhelmed by it *At Thill's Grave*, the poem to which the later letter provides a precise commentary. The tears, which he cannot hold back in the shadow of the elder tree, are doubled—for an incomprehensible reason, doubly shed tears.

When it came to *The Churchyard*, Hölderlin had left mourning and tears behind and with them the conflict in whose dynamic the clear-sighted words of June 1799 belong: "Man," as he wrote in the previous paragraph of the same letter, "in order to live and be active, must unify both in his breast, mourning and hope, cheerfulness and ugliness. And this is, as I believe, also the attitude of the Christian. And this is the way you [mother] have also understood it." That justification with respect to religious duty to which the mother wants to bind her son distorts melancholy, as melancholy distorts mourning whose source it displaces. Thus in the fragment, which begins with the words "From the abyss namely,"

"A wild hill" is mentioned, where "over streams bends lithe/A walnut tree . . . and berries, like coral/Hang on stems over tubes of wood"—a fragment that permits us to group together allusions whose topology is pacified within the restricted domain, and behind the protective wall, of *The Churchyard*.[31]

The identification with the mother explains the melancholy of the poet. The psychotic turn of this melancholia is caused by a mourning for the father taken over from the mother, thereby barring access to him—a double loss. This side of the story is easy to see. For the expulsion of the father from the oedipal situation removes not only an unwanted rival but also, and above all, as Foucault has explained in his synopsis, the protection he offers in separation: "when he proclaims *the law*, he binds therewith the experience of space, social rules, and language to a more comprehensive order. Immediately and all at once appears in this order the space according to whose measure the rhythm of being-there and being-away is constituted . . . "[32] Foucault makes plausible what in the language of Lacanian orthodoxy means expulsion out of the 'symbolic order.'[33] So far, so good Hölderlin's case is an example, "clear from the outside, but ambiguous under the surface," as Foucault makes us aware. And what is at stake here is nothing but the *repudiation*, the 'foreclusion' of the 'Name of the Father,' and that is not the mere *absence* of a factual father but the failure of the symbolic father. Namely, in registering it "not under the rubric of perception or of image" but rather "in the rubric of the signifier," Foucault follows the trail of Lacan.

Laplanche's study is devoted, not more and not less, to demonstrating the decisive concept of 'foreclusion' with the help of Hölderlin and within the confines of the paradigm constituted by his case history. Laplanche is perfectly aware of the methodological difficulties that a poet's work poses for psychiatric evaluation—difficulties that Foucault more decisively than Laplanche wants to solve in declaring poetry the privileged source of madness. According to Foucault, this value of poetry as a source of madness is due to a paradoxical awareness of itself that creates space for itself in the work, in it alone is legible.[34] The exemplary self-revelation of the subject, not only of this but of every subject in the limits of its decenteredness, its constitution in signifiers, is owing in the end to a complicity or, less criminal, to an epistemological interest shared by psychoanalytical and aesthetic discourse; against this Foucault wants to do justice to the epistemological surplus, if not excess, of the poetical work (a surplus hardly worth mentioning in Foucault's later work).

Laplanche tries hard to include this surplus of the poetic text in his analysis: "What is missing when Schreber says the word father," Laplanche admits, "and quite certainly he expresses it, is still to be determined." Also in Hölderlin's oeuvre the word 'father,' "le nom de *père*," returns frequently enough and is "rich in connotations." "But, as far as the real father of Hölderlin is concerned, the passages in the correspondence are very sparse and always determined to revive a formless shadow arisen from Hades."[35] However, the shadows of the elder tree, which were addressed at Thill's grave, stand in the plural like the fathers for whom the involuntary, incomprehensible tears were shed. Even if we concede to Laplanche that the early, pathetic staging of *Die Meinigen* reveals little more than the mentioning of the father that here in fact is introduced "in the name of the father," Laplanche conversely would have to concede that the implications of the metaphor thus constituted finds a subtle representation and application in the poem *At Thill's Grave*. What delineates itself in Hölderlin's poetry in the representation of this discovery, which Laplanche apparently makes, is once more an allegory, an allegory of reading similar to that of the 'purloined letter,' a diagnosis that offers itself almost automatically and requires a diagnosis of its own.

Let's recapitulate. The genealogy of the 'Name of the Father' in Hölderlin—"Master of worlds!" and "Eternally true father!" (*Die Meinigen*, first and fourth stanzas); "Oh father! dear blessed one!" (*At Thill's Grave*, second stanza)—identifies in the name of God and in substitute for the real father the constitution of a, of *the* metaphor: *the law* and the rule of *substitution*, according to which "in the name of the father," the law establishes itself in the real father and constitutes beyond his limited existence the 'symbolic father.'[36] Thus one can hardly say that Hölderlin had no concept of the symbolic father—unless by that one wanted to say that he had been unable to have a concept of it to the extent that he had developed a metaphor of it.[37] This is not far from a quotation Laplanche takes from Lacan. Lacan had spoken of "the flood of treatments of the signifier, from where the growing havoc of the imaginary issues forth, until the level is reached at which signifier and signified stabilize themselves in the delirious metaphor."[38]

What was necessary in the trivial sense, according to Lacan in the disillusionment of the sentence immediately following, was not "le père du suject" but a thoroughly real one, a "père réel," anyone, as he punningly says, Un-père. Schiller, according to Laplanche, was also predestined for this role and was in the position "to furnish Hölderlin some symbolic elements." This would be relevant, if Hölderlin had not acquired those elements long before. (The myth of Phaeton prescribed by Schiller would have rather functioned as a barely veiled threat). Whatever one may thus accept as the fatal catalyst, "the unmastered return of the phallus under the symbolically equivalent form of the natural child," as postulated by Laplanche (the child born by Marianne Kirms, as later research has found out), could have been only disastrous in view of Schiller's real presence.[39] No such return can be traced in Hölderlin's work with the signifying material, but could only be postulated as a "missing link."

Lacan's 'métaphore délirante,' on the other hand, carries the features of a vivification openly at work in hallucinatory moments of poetic illusion (more precisely rhetorical illusio). The poem Andenken has been credited with such a moment of lively presentification. The complicity between the discourses of psychoanalysis and literature discussed by Foucault and Derrida has found in the convergence of delirious metaphor and living metaphor its most peculiar but also its most questionable form of compromise. In it Henrich's Gang des Andenkens and Ricoeur's Métaphore vive go together with

Heidegger's reading of Hölderlin, where the latter, *on the way to language*, regards "words, like flowers" (in *Bread and Wine*) as the "awakening of the widest gaze." In Ricoeur's translation and conclusion: "it makes the world appear. For isn't it this that makes the metaphor alive?"[40] Nothing in the liveliness of appearance separates these living appearances from delirium. However, both *métaphore délirante* and *métaphore vive* cannot be brought to agreement, but rather the appearance of their similiarity inscribes in both *ex negativo* the difference that would be lost if one would force them into congruence. Even if the figtree in *Andenken* also carries the features of living metaphor, this is only a souvenir whose remembrance merely quotes a performance of vivification in contrast to which the poem is constituted, and makes a difference as a poem. Against this, the delirious metaphor would be a result of stabilization and that means here simply the result of a confusion of signifiers, repressed but pressing in metaphor, with the obvious signified. It would be nothing but an artificially animated, ghostly catachresis, *abusio* of a vivification that is exposed in 'dead metaphor.'[41]

Contrary to all expectations of psychotic destiny put forward in the analysis of Laplanche, this mock resolution of signifying delirium is in Hölderlin's *Churchyard* repudiated and left behind. The philological fact that the name of the father is "reticent," as Sattler says, and that, in other words, the elder is not explicitly named but rather brought as appearance before the eyes, this proves no *métaphore délirante* in which the signified would help the repressed signifiers to return. The presumption of such a delirium can only be understood as *métaphore vive*: as relapse or regression to a type of metaphor that *Andenken* had left behind as sad trope, lost illusion. One sees how a certain reading of Hölderlin, in particular the late work before his psychosis, immediately calls for and demands the diagnosis of this psychosis. And it appears as a helpful point of the Lacanian concept of metaphor, in particular its psychotic specification of *métaphore délirante*, to have exposed this complicity of philology and psychiatry. In the end, Hölderlin, as can be read in the poem *The Churchyard*, had grown out of the illusion of the "insistence of letters."

This last illusion of "logocentrism" is the hardest; to see through it means to admit a virtual undecidability. The oscillation between *métaphore vive* and *métaphore délirante* leads to an aesthetic valorization that upgrades the illusionary vivification of the delirium and raises received beauty beyond the borders of the experienceable to the realm of the sublime—in short, madness as a referential short-circuit localized in the sphere of the 'other.' Undecidability can only be shown and exposed in a configuration of pretexts. It can be captured in the "retrait of metaphor" and read from the krypt of the withdrawn. What bears fruit in *The Churchyard* is catachresis, dead metaphor, that is arranged with the hallucinatory certainty of a metaphor alive. And what is called to the stage in this metaphor is the name of the father, but a father who, implicated in the peace of this place, *is* no longer part of this metaphor.

Ludo Verbeeck has given to the formal pattern of branches hanging over blossoming ground a meaning that we find again in *The Churchyard*: "Image of the empty place."[42] It offers itself in the poem *Der Winkel von Hardt* (*The Shelter at Hardt*):

> Hinunter sinket der Wald,
> Und Knospen ähnlich, hängen
> Einwärts die Blätter, denen
> Blüht unten auf ein Grund . . .

> *Down sinks the forest,*
> *And, like buds, hang*
> *Inward the leaves*
> *Against which blooms a ground . . .*

More radical even is the image of the empty place in *The Churchyard*: "on that grey wall/Where yonder a tree hangs with fruit." Böschenstein was the first to make the audacious assertion that in Hölderlin's last poems "*nothing* is perceived," namely nothing made visual other than the "passage of time."[43] But this insight was too little for him and had to be reconnected with a theological remainder. For Böschenstein, this passage of time is "the clothing of eternity, whose holiness [remains] graspable as pure, empty duration." What, however, remains comprehensible in the baroque after-image of overextended transcendence that the *Churchyard* evokes in a last allegory is solely the this-worldly nature whose completed fullness stands for nothing more than the staying away of transcendence: "and being pious, undisturbed" (last line).

The elder tree, "wild elder," which has "bloomed around" the garden of the father, stands early in Hölderlin's work for the name of the father (in the poem *The Wanderer*); later we find it again in the elder tree in whose shadow ungraspable mourning surfaces (*At Thill's Grave*); it temporalizes "black dewy fruits" whose tangible presence "on that grey wall" no longer represent an unhappy reminder but undisturbed forgetting that has taken its place. For *The Churchyard* is not the "image of an empty place" because of any resurrection taking place there, attested by church officials. The grave is empty, but the name of the father in the figure of the tree is nothing but the image of this emptiness, from which his return is not to be expected. The adherence of the *same* with whose unreachable presence and graspable absence Hölderlin had been possessed, according to Foucault; similarly, the "trust" that, according to Bertaux, had its lasting fulfillment in Diotima, found its last rest in the emptiness of the image. As in the remembrance of the poem *Andenken*, the 'institution' (*Stiften*) performed by the poet signifies an insistence on those marks of memory whose fullness arises out of the emptiness of their reference. *The Churchyard* signifies in the progression of this process the last stage of separation from the scheme of allegory. The happy life of undisturbed contemplation—no longer bothered by a clergyman's talk, by the name of the father, and the care of the mother—also escapes the empathy of interpreters. Marked by a renunciation and abandonment hard to imagine, Hölderlin expects from the happy life something beyond the understanding of those who psychoanalyze his withdrawal: in the spare frames of empty images, the fullness of things called forth from nothing.

Mourning Becomes Melancholia: The Leaves of Books

Nor let the beetle, nor
the death-moth be
Your mournful Psyche—[1]
—John Keats

Ode on Melancholy
(Keats and Locke)

Freud's *Beyond the Pleasure Principle,* one is tempted to say, leads mourning beyond melancholia. Such an outcome for "Mourning and Melancholia," however, is less conclusive than the universal 'beyond' may suggest. Mourning defies definition just as melancholia, its unworkable other, defies mourning.[2] At a first glance, it looks as if, according to Freud, melancholia leads beyond mourning, and it seems to be the pleasure principle that is left behind in melancholia rather than in mourning. At a second glance, though, there is a narcissistic relapse to be observed in melancholia that accounts for the inability to mourn. Melancholia would thus be the dead end of the pleasure principle, while the ability to mourn would lead beyond in the sense that it not only comes to terms with but acknowledges that which remains inaccessible to those terms—the human condition of mortality.

"Melancholy in this sense," we read in Burton's *Anatomy of Melancholy* from 1621, "is the character of mortality."[3] This character or imprint of mortality takes the place of the former *character crucis*, which was the imprint of baptism, and leaves the promise of an afterlife to the anatomy of dead letters. It foreshadows a beyond of other dimensions, the dimension of the 'unconscious.' Freud's distinction between mourning and melancholia, which describes the difference in terms of unconscious and conscious losses—conscious in the case of mourning, unconscious in the case of melancholia— still bears the mark of common sense, of "moderation" and "just reason," as Burton had required (II/180). Within Freud's theory of the unconscious, this distinction represents a heuristic move rather than a systematic step in coming to terms with a certain pathological disposition, melancholia, as opposed to a certain normal behavior, mourning. The normality of this behavior is qualified by the understanding of an evidently decisive loss, which *causes* grief; while the pathology of melancholia is above all characterized by an apparently *causeless*, and therefore incomprehensible, condition of depression. As "Mourning and Melancholia" proceeds, however, the pragmatics of the problem at hand are undermined and a more fundamental question is raised, which leads beyond mere adaptation to reality. In the case of loss, this adaptation is brought about by the 'work of mourning,' as Freud very pointedly calls it. Since life is haunted by losses and, as survival, is established on the premises of losses, the work of mourning turns out to be nothing less than the reality principle itself operative in the overcoming of losses.

The phenomenology of mourning, implied rather than overcome by Freud's distinction, has been further developed by one of his closest readers, Benjamin, in his book on the *Origin of German Tragic Drama*, in his discussion of the *Trauerspiel*, which literally translates as "play of mourning" instead of the "work of mourning." There is more to this casual opposition than meets the eye, since it is the melancholy constitution of the world rather than the successful adaptation to reality that provokes Benjamin's "theory of mourning" (his words):

Each sentiment, or mood, is directed towards, and depends upon, an a priori subject, the representation of which is its phenomenology. The theory of mourning . . . thus can only be developed in the description of the world [the 'life-world,' as phenomenologists would say; the 'death-world,' as Benjamin would rather have it] that reveals itself to the eye of the melancholy man.[4]

Melancholy, according to Benjamin, is the basic modern (baroque) disposition to which a theory of mourning has to conform, the basic 'concept of (modern) reality,' as Blumenberg has put it, a *Stimmung* or *Gestimmtheit*, as the more romantically minded *Jargon of Authenticity* has called it.[5] Benjamin's theory of mourning, however, does not just give us another regional phenomenology of yet another mode of 'being in time.' The phenomenology of melancholy, as the very subject of Benjamin's theory of mourning, implies a temporality of its subject that, moreover, reflects the historicality of phenomenology. The phenomenology of melancholy, one could say, is caught within the melancholy of phenomenology—as Burton already knew. Thus the origin of melancholy marks the origin of phenomenology; phenomenology is the result of and proper to the melancholy eye. The historicality of this episteme, to put it in terms of Foucault's 'archaeology' of the same formation, is presupposed by Freud's distinction. Freud's distinction, consequently, turns from an anthropological, though heuristical, fiction into a historical concept. Under the auspices of a theory of mourning, phenomenology reveals a historical 'a priori,' which is described by Benjamin as the melancholy condition of subjectivity in a modern world; the modern 'I' as reflected by the melancholy eye.

Rather than go further into the metacritical problems of phenomenology and psychoanalysis, I shall elaborate the theory of mourning within the frame of a 'historical phenomenology.'[6] As the fate of Burton's *Anatomy* shows, this project is by no means alien to literary studies but can be only based upon criticism in the strict sense. Frye, therefore, is able to translate the *Anatomy of Melancholy* into the *Anatomy of*

Criticism, with the obvious implication that criticism performs upon texts anatomically, thereby presupposing the death of its objects as well as the melancholy of the performing critic—the "mortification of the works," as Benjamin says.[7] Like Benjamin's book on the Trauerspiel, Frye's Anatomy is a book about allegory as a "principle of structure," as the New Critics used to say.[8] Although one has to qualify this use of the term structure, since Foucault's archaeology makes clear that the age of similitudes and resemblances, of allegory, was, in fact, a pre-structuralist age.[9] What can be learned from Foucault's archaeology of structuralism is, above all, that the preceding episteme organized knowledge allegorically, according to the resemblance of "four similitudes." Allegory not only becomes the critical equivalent of literary structure, but was 'structure' in the prestructural age, and was 'representation' before scientific representation came about in the Age of Reason. The metaphor anatomy indicates the new prevalence of analytical operations, of criticism in the new sense, over the older techniques of allegorical commentaries. An anatomy of criticism thus turns out to be an anatomy of allegory in the post-allegorical episteme of representation. What can be learned from Benjamin's phenomenology of melancholy is, on the other hand, that the allegorical structure of texts—analyzed structurally, that is, anatomically—presupposes the end of that allegorical age of resemblance and the impertinence of the similitudes. Reading the new way, that is, critically, now means a structural procedure that becomes melancholy in that it mortifies its objects and consequently perceives them as dead texture. Reading is melancholy in its 'perception' of a materiality of texts, in the contemplation of the dead letter, as there is, in the words of one of Benjamin's baroque sources, "nothing more mournful than books."[10]

According to Benjamin, the theory of mourning implies a theory of reading as the mournful perception of the world; as in de Man, who read Benjamin more and more closely, the theory of reading becomes a theory of mourning, of unreadability and the impossibility of mourning—melancholia. The question is less how much mourning is done in reading than how much reading is needed in mourning. Mourning becomes the term for what reading might be all about: a coming to terms with what is on the page, just as what is (left) on the page was a coming to terms with what was not on the page before. The 'error in mourning' that separates melancholia from 'true mourning' would thus be an error in coming to terms with what is on the page by overleaping the fact that it is on the page *only*. Consequently, the impossibility of mourning becomes the exemplary instance of the unreadability of writing.

The paradigmatic case I would like to investigate here needs no lengthy introduction, though it does perhaps need a methodological warning that no thematic approach is intended. That Keats's "Ode" is "On Melancholy" does not suffice to make it a preferable or exemplary instance of the history of mourning and melancholia. The history of grief and mourning that has been recently elucidated with respect to the English Renaissance Elegy is a good example of the impasses common to histories of ideas in the field of psycho-history, that is, the confusion of thematic and formalist approaches to which this topic is highly susceptible.[11] Certainly, the history of the associated commonplaces (*topoi*) of grief and consolation as well as the generic features of the elegy as the very genre of mourning are of the greatest interest for the hermeneutical frames of 'understanding' mourning in or by poems.[12] Consequently, the paradoxical outcome of a historical survey along those lines shows a growing lack of understanding, a repression almost of mourning in texts *on* mourning—a coming to terms on the page, that is, where there was no coming to terms for texts, an impossibility of mourning that had to be compensated for by consolation. Stanley Fish's reading of *Lycidas*—"A Poem Finally Anonymous"—tries to make a virtue out of this impasse. The breaking of form, of the generic unity of the elegy as the genre of both mourning and consolation, becomes manifest in *Lycidas*, when the speaker says to the apostrophized berries, "I am sorry to have to do this to you"; and what he is even sorrier about is that "something . . . has been done to him," as Fish aptly points out: what is left to him, in other words, "What he can do, and very effectively, is to . . . disassociate himself from the [poetic] failures he continues to expose [in this poem]."[13] The withdrawal of the poet into final anonymity, however, leaves the poem finally unconsoled.[14] It approaches, in the understanding of Freud's phenomenological critics (from Benjamin to Derrida), the impossibility of mourning. Keats, whose *Ode* draws heavily upon both Burton and *Lycidas*, represents something like the final instance of the same stage in the (pre-)history of mourning and melancholia, though certainly not in the figure of the romantic hero that Milton's lyrical voice could not, and Keats's voice would not, be. A nearly anonymous voice turns against the muse that cannot be silenced but can be named, exposed, and imprisoned in the poem, *Melancholy*.

It is in Locke's *Essay Concerning Human Understanding* that we find a hunch, a first idea of Freud's distinction, in one of the supplementary examples he added to the fourth edition of 1701. There he lists, under the heading of "wrong connexion of ideas," cases of "incurable sorrow":

> The death of a child that was the daily delight of its mother's eyes, and a joy of her soul, rends from her heart the whole comfort of her life, and gives her all the torment imaginable. . . . Till time has by disuse separated the sense of that enjoyment and its loss, from the idea of the child returning to her memory, all representations, though ever so reasonable, are in vain; and therefore some in whom the union between these ideas is never dissolved, spend their lives in mourning, and carry an incurable sorrow to their graves.[15]

What Locke calls "an incurable sorrow," and what Freud came to distinguish as melancholy from mourning, stems from an inability to "dissolve" a wrong connection of ideas, for example the mother's outdated expectation that keeps "the child returning to her memory." It is memory that accounts for melancholia, according to Locke, through a misled memory of an outdated association of ideas. Consequently, Hölderlin's account of an "error in mourning" reports the death of

Mnemosyne (memory) while Keats's *Ode* begins with an ostentatious turning away from Lethe ("forgetting"): "No, no, go not to Lethe . . . " (l. 1).

Burton's *Anatomy*, which is one of the sources or intertexts of Keats's first stanza, not with respect to Lethe but to the enumerated causes of suicide that lead to Lethe, and to drugs leading to forgetting, had mentioned among the causes of melancholy "Death of friends, Losses, &c.," but without obviously getting near the point Locke at least approaches and "associates." "In the labyrinth of accidental causes," Burton thinks, "loss and death of friends may challenge a first place." This cause appears to him as merely "accidental," since its melancholy effect appears arbitrary—an effect that is very painfully described in a large variety of cases: "still, still, still, that good father, that good son, that good wife, that dear friend runs in their minds; . . . all the year long, as Pliny complains to Romanus, Methinks I see Virginius, I hear Virginius, I talk to Virginius, &c." (I/357–58). The description is pertinent in that it faithfully represents the repetitive force within melancholia, but the underlying mechanism appears to be both evident and mysterious at the same time. The cause in this case explains nothing, remains apparently accidental in that it triggers a behavior that cannot be simply reduced to this cause because it reproduces the cause that produces it and thus appears to be causeless, like the "melancholy fit" that foreshadows what later came to be known in Baudelaire as 'spleen.' Burton, it seems, describes what we more easily identify as an error in mourning, but he shows it rather than explains it, and, while showing rather than explaining it, does so very effectively.

Locke already approximates the theoretically manifest distinction of Freud, though we have to be very careful not to over-read him; his associationist psychology does not anticipate psychoanalysis but rather heightens its explanatory effects. The ability to "dissolve," as Locke has it, is obviously not synonymous with repression, where nothing is dissolved but where the unresolved remains active. Thus we can read Locke as a theoretical rationalization of Burton's description, but not as an explanation for what is at stake in Hölderlin,

Keats, or Baudelaire. They, however, presuppose the topicality of enlightened commonplace psychology.[16] Freud, on the other hand, relates to romanticism as Locke to Burton, though one would have to qualify the differences of these relations considerably.[17] Keats, finally, as Hölderlin before him, marks the threshold to be crossed. Technically speaking, this crossing over reveals its anticipatory quality in the way it relates to, and comes to terms with, the poetical tradition it leaves behind, although not without recalling it once more intertextually. Coming to terms thus proves to be a coming to tropes with what had already been tropes before, a retroping of already existing allegories as poetical failures of representations. There is a new kind of intertextuality to be observed, which makes a difference in terms of mourning and melancholia.

The transtextual references in Keats's *Ode* are easy to identify, perhaps too easy. The first stanza recalls Burton's *Anatomy* and in doing so resumes Milton's refutation in *Lycidas* of the elegiac mode of consolation—at the same time, however, alluding to the first elegy of Ovid's *Tristia*. I quote from a late nineteenth-century translation which keeps prosaically to its seventeenth-century model, Saltonstall's *Tristia* (the addressee being the book sent home by Ovid as the witness of his fate):

> Let not the hyacinth array you in its purple tints; . . . Let not your title be inscribed in vermilion, nor let your leaves be prepared with the oil of the cedar; and do not wear whitened extremities [ends, or tops, that is, "covers"] with a blackened page. Let these appliances be the ornaments of more fortunate books: it benefits you to keep your fate in remembrance. And let not the two sides of your leaves be polished . . . And be not ashamed of your blots: he who beholds them will be sensible that they were caused by my tears.[18]

Habent sua fata libelli, but the fate of this one is to give evidence of the fate of its author, to represent his melancholy over the loss of his country (the *nostalgia* for heaven, according to the allegorical *interpretatio christiana*), as Keats's poem represents—that is, quotes—the *melancholia* of a tradition that failed in coming to terms, in terms of consolation, with this loss as well. Summing up this loss in the representation of its associated hopes, Keats applies Burton's anatomy and produces a texture that distances structurally what had been substantially at stake. This 'texture,' according to New Critical procedures, is submitted to a rational 'argument,' the logic of which borders on parody.[19] Irony surfaces in places of grammatical impertinence, semantical inconsistences, 'ambiguity,' as Empson has called it.[20] I follow his advice and come to the following first reading of the ode.

The dramatically staged warning, enumerating Burton's commonplaces, hides an urgent anxiety about suicide under the ironic surface of a parody. The ambiguity involved represents the same repetitive momentum as exemplified by Burton: "No, no, go not . . . ," an anxiety not of influence but of its opposite, forgetting: " . . . not to Lethe." It counteracts the suicidal tendencies of melancholy, and, taking countermeasures, makes the "Ode *to* Melancholy," as one would expect, into an *Ode on Melancholy*: Melancholy is not addressed but dealt with, and the antidote in dealing with melancholy, as invented in romanticism, is irony.[21] It is a rather shaky irony, though, but effective enough to wrest from the second stanza the temporary pleasure of an apparently natural setting, as opposed to the seemingly mythical setting of the first stanza. The dialectics of both brings the initial warning to a final exhortation, we read in a good many paraphrases of the poem's argument: it is, in the commentary by Miriam Allott, "a characteristic Keatsian statement about the necessary relationship between joy and sorrow. True melancholy," the summary goes on, is "felt only"—that is, "experienced" in the true sense—in the dialectics of both, joy and sorrow.[22] The "Temple of Delight," consequently, is seen as a late *locus amoenus* of the romantic quest, where the coincidence of joy and sorrow is worshipped, not sorrow cured.[23]

What sets the ode apart from this pattern, however, is the ambivalent irony, the carefully preserved detachment from experience, which makes it an almost experimental device. It is the "melancholy fit" only, the manic opposite of the preced-

ing depression, that is ironically exposed; the splenetic rather
than serene outcome which projects its own raving desire onto
the desired beloved—a projection that is almost the opposite
of empathic experience. Just as Burton's descriptive phenomenology served as a pretext for an all-too-ambivalent irony to
overcome depression, this very depression now—in a reaction-
formation against mere phenomenology—serves as pretext
for an almost manic acting out of a perverted desire: "if thy
mistress some rich anger shows,/Imprison her soft hand,
and let her rave" (ll. 18–19). What makes her eyes "peerless" is not their glance looking back, but their value as an
introject—how they mirror back, reflect the projected, narcissistic I. This mediation of the two extremes of pathological
melancholia (mania and depression) leads in Keats's third
stanza into a petrifying allegorization of the avoided addressee
of the ode, Melancholy, which turns from the formerly addressed muse into an abstraction beyond the means of apostrophe. As we know from Freud's account of melancholia,
abstractions like this one always stand for a loss, a loss that in
this case the muse is unable to account for.

The irony of allusion, though, had managed to quote the
loss: "She dwells with Beauty" (l. 21) obviously parodies Byron's "She walks in beauty"; "Beauty that must die," as Keats
continues, while Byron calls her "like the night," and we learn
later that she "appeared in mourning, with dark spangles on
her dress."[24] The grammatical subject of Keats's sentence,
however, which seemed to refer to the object of the preceding
stanza, the mistress of perverted desire, turns out to be the ob-
jectifying instance, the goddess Melancholy herself. This allegorical result of the poem is amplified by another quotation
taken from the mouth of another poet, "his poet" for Keats,
Shakespeare (by way of Horace).[25] In Sonnet 31 we find the following apostrophe, not only to the subject, the "young man,"
but at the same time to the vehicle, the poem itself: "Thou art
the grave where buried love doth live,/Hung with the trophies
of my lovers gone."[26]

The result of the consummation of love, the using up of
the beloved within the abuse of melancholy ("feed deep, deep

upon her peerless eyes," l. 20), makes the poet himself a "trophy," cloudy like the spleen (the "weeping cloud," l. 12). "His soul" (a "death-moth" rather than "Psyche's" butterfly) turns into one of Melancholy's "trophies hung," just as the addressee appeared in Shakepeare's sonnet as the "grave" for the poet's "lovers gone." The difference is decisive and deserves a closer look; its differentiating momentum not only re-tropes but de-tropes Shakespeare's 'image.' The melancholy poet consciously digs his own grave or, rather, in writing it he tries to escape it; and in not addressing it properly, as the genre and the model of Shakespeare would have required, he holds back, pretending, in fact, to be someone else, shifting from "feed deep" to "His soul" in an ironic splitting of his lyrical voice. No lyrical I is left, only a lyrical eye observing itself as an other on whom to blame the consequential "shall," the future "trophy," the poem that is left on the page, "saved from drowning" (as Barthelme put it) in "the wakeful anguish of the soul" (l. 10).[27]

This first, preliminary reading, drawn from Empson's short but far-reaching remarks, is still rendered in a paraphrase and thus is guilty of the heresy of paraphrase; it has to be rephrased in a second, more structural reading. The paraphrase still does, at least attempts to, 'understand' the poem; it follows, not without close attention to its texture, the logical argument established in the text: "Go not to Lethe" (whatever this means, drugs or suicide), but "when the melancholy fit shall fall" (l. 11), make the best of it, though it's not the best; "imprison," though you'll be the prisoner, and the imprisoned object of desire shall make you the subject matter of your own disposition (as Shakespeare had, in a memorable way, symbolized the narcissistic constitution of the writing subjectivity). This understanding of the poem has now to be investigated according to its condition of possibility, that is, in the paradoxical case of melancholia, according to the condition of the impossibility of mourning.

Irony here is the means of coming to terms with melancholia, though the term we actually arrive at, *irony*, is by no means clear, and something like Burke's 'mystic oxymoron' may seem more appropriate.[28] What used to be and no longer is an "Ode *to*" has turned into an "Irony *on*." The application of irony to melancholy retropes, or refashions, another super-imposition that was the work of melancholy on allegory; it does not deconstruct the work of melancholy, as does, in fact, Keats's poem. The loss of eschatology, the collapse of the ty-pological perspective of allegory, the destruction of its *schema* or *figura*, results in and is prolonged by the melancholy de-scribed by Benjamin.[29] The prohibition of a prolonged mourn-ing, as melancholy had been conceived of until the baroque, had turned into an inability to mourn in this life: "He that feares death, or mournes it, in the just,/Shows of the resurrec-tion little trust," runs an orthodox epigram *Of Death* by Ben Jonson.[30] Thus the inability to mourn was supposed to prove faith in the promised afterlife, as well as to show the same within this life. Melancholy petrifies this attitude of an out-dated allegorical order of things into what de Man calls an 'an-thropomorphism' of the underlying trope, allegory.[31]

De Man supplements Benjamin's model of melancholy in that he analyzes the melancholy of allegory as an "anthropo-morphism of trope." Anthropomorphism, however, is a hermeneutical term, not a rhetorical one; as an instrument of enlightened critique of religion, it counteracts rather than sup-plements a certain pre-critical use of dogmatic rhetoric. It thus reflects very precisely the historicality of the problem it sys-tematically investigates. In the Kantian tradition (including Nietzsche), anthropomorphism is a rhetorical fallacy, by which the allegorical potential of literature is frozen within the dogmatic frames of theology. Melancholy, one could say, is the allegorical name for the death of allegory. It allegorically "reinscribes," as Benjamin would say, *Allegory* on the dead face, the skull, of what had been allegory before. But it also gives a face to the lost object and presents a voice from beyond the grave. As a withdrawal symptom it manifests itself in an almost hallucinatory way. It testifies, finally, to the loss of hermeneutical control over the inherited allegorical frame of reference. Irony, on the other hand, is yet another and, in fact, the older anthropomorphism of trope. Since Quintilian's dou-ble definition of irony as both trope and state of mind (Socrates being its personification), irony exemplifies paradigmatically the anthropomorphic condition of tropological discourse or, more precisely, the anthropomorphic state of the tropological condition of discourse. It thematizes as well as criticizes; it disrupts as well as prolongs what is going on. The irony of Keats's ode thus not only thematizes but criticizes melancholy; it disrupts the genre of the ode as well as prolongs its writing. In the development of Keats's writing, it is the ode, and not the elegy, that proves to be the genre of mourning rather than consoling, whereas elegy seems to be absorbed by melancholy rather than the work of mourning.

Earl Wasserman in his classic book on Keats's major poems described a similar conflict of interpretations (though not of anthropomorphisms of trope), a similar detachment from (or almost deconstruction of) what he plausibly called the "empathic participation in the life of the images" as established in the *Ode on a Grecian Urn* and destroyed by the *Ode to a Nightingale*: "The thematic materials of the two odes, we shall see, are the same; but what blends organically in the *Ode on a Grecian Urn* disintegrates in this ode; what is seen in its immortal aspects in the former is seen in its mortal aspects in the latter."[32] The *Ode on Melancholy*, which does not make it into Wasserman's selection of major poems, performs a similar "disintegration" (Wasserman's term) on the *Ode to Psyche*, which Wasserman admits he never "learned to read." Wasserman's intuitions supplement each other. The disintegration works in this pair of related poems in autoreversal to the one analyzed by him—in the reversal of an "Ode *to*" into an "Ode *on*." What counts here is the deconstructive power of the one text over the other, a mutual relation, moreover, in which one anthropomorphism replaces the other to be self-deconstructed in this very replacement. Irony, in this case, does more, in that it establishes a permanent movement that postpones indefinitely while wittingly keeping alive the dangerous impact of the postponed. Irony, in overcoming melancholy, makes melancholy the anthropomorphism of trope that it used to be under the reign of a different 'rhetoric of temporality.' In Keats's *Ode on Melancholy*, the address to an immortal soul, Psyche, is reduced to a meditation on its mortality, its limited availability, and final unreadability.[33]

What distinguishes this *meditatio mortis* is the doubt it casts upon the genre of consolation and its melancholy condition. This meditation comes into being only as the par-ody of the genre it meditates in its incapability; it has, as Keats pointedly names it, 'negative capability.'

As far as the tradition thus destroyed is concerned, it is the very allusion to and resuming of the destroyed that construes a new, though very precarious 'meaning'—a truly ambivalent outcome that makes the *Ode* truly an ode *on Melancholy*. I restrict myself to the Shakespeare sonnet, which at the end of the ode is not just alluded to but played with. Keats resumes in these lines what Shakespeare presents in his sonnet: the narcissistic pose by which the poet reviews his poem as an assembly of lost loves, impersonated by the notorious "young man"; an assembly of "trophies" not of success but of failure, impersonated by the infamous addressee of the poem, the poem. Keats adds to these victims of the poet the poet himself as the victim of poetry or rather of the muse that melancholy became of poetry. Doubling the Shakespearean doubling of the addressee of the poem by the poem itself, Keats doubles the subject of the poem, the poet, by what is subjected to it, the poet himself.

Sonnet 31, as Shakespeare's editor Stephen Booth points out, is "the second of two *exempla* for the homely proverb, 'In love is no lack.'"[34] It finally proves how his poem, the sonnet, is in lack of love, and how this lack of loving made it what it became through lacking: a "grave" with "trophies," haunted by "images"—that is, "ghosts in the machine" in both senses, the Cartesian sense as well as the "machine to think with," which is the poem.[35] Keats thus manipulates the tenor of the vehicle at hand, provoking something like a "ghost dance." The 'empathic participation' (Wasserman) they trigger in vain cuts the "lover" and his love into "parts," as Shakespeare says, and makes up the parts of the poem. For Shakespeare the poem presents the losses of love in the ghostly appearance of "images"; for Keats the same act of presentation is represented as melancholy and "reigned" by melancholy. For Shakespeare the loss is overcome and "reigned" by poetry, for Keats this mourning remains untrue and consequently rejoices in melancholy. What was for Shakespeare the pretext of writing becomes the impossibility of the same writing for Keats, though an ironically and ambiguously joyful one ("Joy's grape," l. 28), as it was for Shakespeare a sad one (Keats's "sadness of her might," l. 29).[36]

Keats identifies melancholy as the necessary implication and historical consequence of what one could judge, from his perspective, as the natural narcissism of Shakespeare's poetry. Read from his modern (romantic) and, as far as Freud is concerned, from a postromantic (postmodern) perspective, Shakespeare's text becomes the perfect exemplification of the melancholy constitution of 'subjectivity,' a subjectivity that is poetical in that it is self-productive—in that it creates its *self*, and while creating itself as *it*-self, detaches itself from *its* self, thereby exposing the condition of its existence on the page and beyond the page. A fictive identity, as the poetic dimension on the page (as text) from now on becomes the model of the 'subject' (our selves, our discipline).[37]

The psychoanalytic hypothesis of the narcissistic constitution of the subject on the model of introjected objects finds its early modern, 'baroque' (in Benjamin's sense) point in poems like Sonnet 31—though we were hardly able to read it that way without having read Keats before. Benjamin points out that the baroque melancholy eye presupposes, even entails, the death of the contemplated object in order to save it eternally and thereby achieve salvation for the subject as well. As Keats's reading and retuning of Shakespeare's sonnet show, the latter hope remains hopeless, and even the melancholy self-reflection of the fictive melancholy self, the self-exposing destruction of the poem, won't do either—except for another, "intensifying and prolonging" poem, one that Keats actually wrote, *To Autumn*, not without having a distressing *Ode on Indolence* to go with it.[38] Keats thus, until his imminent end, nourished the ambivalence at the bottom of his melancholia and followed, in a poetical working through, the repetition compulsion of modern writing.

Notes

Preface to the American Edition

1. Walter Benjamin, *Ursprung des deutschen Trauerspiels* (1928), *Gesammelte Schriften*, vol. 1 (Frankfurt: Suhrkamp, 1974), last pages, 406.

2. Paul de Man, "Anthropomorphism and Trope in the Lyric," *The Rhetoric of Romanticism* (New York: Columbia University Press, 1984), last page, 262.

3. See the Hölderlin chapter in Robert Bernasconi, *The Question of Language in Heidegger's History of Being* (Atlantic Highlands, N. J. : Humanities Press, 1985), 29–47.

4. Bettine Menke, *Sprachfiguren: Name-Allegorie-Bild nach Walter Benjamin* (Munich: Fink, 1991), 206 (my paraphrase).

5. See Cynthia Chase introducing Marjorie Levinson's Introduction to *Keats's Life of Allegory* (Oxford: Blackwell, 1988), in *Romanticism* (London: Longman, 1993), 185.

6. See Cathy Caruth, *Empirical Truths and Critical Fictions* (Baltimore: Johns Hopkins University Press, 1991), 33–43, on Locke; and Barbara Vinken, "Mourning Women: Andromache," *Pequod* 35 (1993): 47–65, on Racine and Baudelaire.

7. See my own brief "Notes on the 'Dialectical Image' (How Deconstructive is It?)," *Diacritics* 22. 3–4 (1992): 70–81.

8. Michel Turnheim, "Hölderlin et la réponse du pire" (Ecole Européenne de Psychanalyse, 1992), translated in his *Freud und der Rest* (Vienna: Turia & Kant, 1993), 163.

9. Michael Fried, *Absorption and Theatricality: Painting and Beholder in the Age of Diderot* (Chicago: Chicago University Press, 1980), 103.

10. See, in this regard, my essay "The Memory of Pictures: Roland Barthes and Augustine on Photography," *Comparative Literature* 45 (1993): 258–279.

Words, Like Flowers: Hölderlin's Late Work

1. Norbert von Hellingrath, *Pindarübertragungen von Hölderlin—Prolegomena zu einer Erstausgabe* (Jena: Diederichs, 1911). The first volume of Hellingrath's Hölderlin-edition to appear in 1916 was vol. 4; it carried the title "Spätwerk" and determined the use of that word. Theodor W. Adorno's "Parataxis" was part of his *Noten zur Literatur, Gesammelte Schriften*, vol. 11 (Frankfurt: Suhrkamp, 1974), and redefined to a large extent what was conceived under the term.

2. See Wilhelm Dilthey, *Das Erlebnis und die Dichtung: Lessing, Goethe, Novalis, Hölderlin* (Leipzig: Teubner, 1906), ending with Hölderlin's *Hälfte des Lebens*; and Karl Jaspers' handbook, *Psychopathologie* (Berlin: Springer, 1922), on the same poem.

3. Peter Szondi, "Über philologische Erkenntnis" (1962), the programmatic introductory essay to his *Hölderlin-Studien* (Frankfurt: Insel, 1967), 30. The Adorno quotation from *Noten zur Literatur* pertains to "Valéry's digressions."

4. Karl Kerényi, "Hölderlins Vollendung," *Hölderlin-Jahrbuch* 8 (1954): 25–45.

5. Peter Szondi, "Der andere Pfeil—Zur Entstehungsgeschichte des hymnischen Spätstils" (1963), *Hölderlin-Studien*: 39. Tr. All translations from the German and French are my own unless otherwise noted.

6. Michel Foucault, "Le *non* du père," *Critique* 178 (1962): 195–209.

7. Hans Lipps, *Untersuchungen zu einer hermeneutischen Logik* (1938), 3rd. ed. (Frankfurt: Klostermann, 1968), 137.

8. D. E. Sattler, "al rovescio: Hölderlin nach 1806," *Le pauvre Holterling* 7 (1984): 17–28.

9. Eugen Gottlob Winkler, "Der späte Hölderlin" (1936), *Eugen Gottlob Winkler*, selected and edited by Walter Jens (Frankfurt: Fischer, 1960), 152.

10. Dieter Henrich, "Hegel und Hölderlin" (1970), *Hegel im Kontext* (Frankfurt: Suhrkamp, 1971), 34.

11. See, tentatively, Claudia Kalász, *Hölderlin—Die poetische Kritik instrumenteller Rationalität* (Munich: Ed. Text + Kritik, 1988), 149. Benjamin fits into the scheme of Horkheimer and Adorno's *Dialectic of Enlightenment* (1944) only in the most general sense.

12. Martin Heidegger, "Das Wesen der Sprache" (1958), *Unterwegs zur Sprache* (Pfullingen: Neske, 1959), 207; respectfully quoted in Paul Ricoeur, *La métaphore vive* (Paris: Seuil, 1975), 361. Heidegger's quotation from Benn extrapolates from the latter's "Probleme der Lyrik" and "Nietzsche–nach fünfzig Jahren. "

13. *Tr.* Hamburger's translation of this line—"Now for it words like flowers leaping alive"—translates Heidegger's reading rather than Hölderlin's wording.

14. See Dirk de Schutter, "Words Like Stones," (*Dis*)*continuities: Essays on Paul de Man*, ed. Luc Herman, Kris Humbeeck, Geert Lernout (Amsterdam: Rodopi, 1990), 99–110. Elaborating my reading of *Mnemosyne*, De Schutter sharpens De Man's refutation of Heidegger, "Structure intentionelle de l'Image romantique" (1960), reprinted in *The Rhetoric of Romanticism* (New York: Columbia University Press, 1984), 4.

15. Jacques Derrida, in a countermove to his answer to Ricoeur's *La métaphore vive*, "Le retrait de la métaphore" (1978), *Psyché—Inventions de l'autre* (Paris: Galilée, 1987), 81.

16. *Tr.* The reference here is to the late romantic novel by Wilhelm Raabe, *Die Akten des Vogelsangs* (Berlin: Janke, 1896).

17. Cynthia Chase, "Viewless Wings–Keats's Ode to a Nightingale" (1985), *Decomposing Figures–Rhetorical Readings in the Romantic Tradition* (Baltimore: Johns Hopkins University Press, 1986), 70. The author alluded to is Milton.

18. See in the meantime Bart Philipsen, *Die List der Einfalt: Nachlese zu Hölderlins später Dichtung* (Munich: Fink, 1995).

19. Walter Benjamin, *Ursprung des deutschen Trauerspiels* (1928), *Gesammelten Schriften*, vol. 1 (Frankfurt: Suhrkamp, 1974), 246.

20. See Theodor W. Adorno's intuition, "Im Jeu de Paume gekritzelt" (1958), *Ohne Leitbild–Parva Aesthetica* (Frankfurt: Suhrkamp, 1967), 43.

21. See Benjamin Hederich, *Gründliches mythologisches Lexicon* (1724), in the edition (used by Hölderlin) enlarged by J. J. Schwaben (Leipzig: Gleditschens Handlung, 1770), s. v. Hesperides 4,6 (1265 ff.).

Mourning Beyond Melancholia: Kryptic Subjectivity

1. Theodor W. Adorno, "Rede über Lyrik und Gesellschaft" (1957), *Noten zur Literatur, Gesammelte Schriften*, vol. 11 (Frankfurt: Suhrkamp, 1974), 59. Cf. Anselm Haverkamp, "Saving the Subject—Randbemerkungen zur Veränderung der Lyrik," *Poetica* 14 (1982): 70–91.

2. Theodor W. Adorno, *Ästhetische Theorie, Gesammelte Schriften*, vol. 7, 133 and, in the following, 169.

3. Wilhelm Dilthey, *Das Erlebnis und die Dichtung* (Leipzig: Teubner, 1906), 46, 159. For the lyric, see the far-reaching and influential consequences of Max Kommerell, *Gedanken über Gedichte*, 2nd ed. (Frankfurt: Klostermann, 1956), 16 ff.

4. Walter Benjamin, "Über einige Motive bei Baudelaire" (1936), *Gesammelte Schriften*, vol. 1 (Frankfurt: Suhrkamp, 1974), 609.

5. Wilhelm Dilthey, "Über die Funktion der Anthropologie in der Kultur des 16. und 17. Jahrhunderts" (1904), *Gesammelte*

Schriften, vol. 2, 5th ed. (Stuttgart: Teubner/Göttingen: Vandenhoeck and Ruprecht, 1957), 416–549, 481.

6. Erving Goffman, *Stigma—Notes on the Management of Spoiled Identity* (1963; Harmondsworth: Penguin, 1968), 129 ff. Cf. Jürgen Habermas, "Stichworte zu einer Theorie der Sozialisation," *Kultur und Kritik* (Frankfurt: Suhrkamp, 1973), 131 ff.

7. "Rede über Lyrik und Gesellschaft," 56 (my emphasis); similarly *Ästhetische Theorie*, 135 ff.

8. See Jacques Derrida, *"La différance"* (1968), *Marges de la philosophie* (Paris: Minuit, 1972), 8, implicitly elaborating the Hölderlinian substratum of this Hegelian motif.

9. See Jacques Lacan, "L'instance de la lettre dans l'inconscient ou la raison depuis Freud" (1957), *Ecrits* (Paris: Seuil, 1966), 511. Cf. Samuel Weber, *Rückkehr zu Freud—Jacques Lacans Entstellung der Psychoanalyse* (Frankfurt, Berlin, Vienna: Ullstein, 1978), 64 ff.

10. Sigmund Freud, "Das Ich und das Es" (1923), *Studienausgabe*, vol. 3 (Frankfurt: Fischer, 1975), 296. Cf. "Triebe und Triebschicksale" (1915), 75–102; and Walter Benjamin, "Schicksal und Charakter" (1921), *Gesammelte Schriften*, vol. 1, 171–79.

11. "Trauer und Melancholie" (1917), *Studienausgabe*, vol. 3, 203.

12. *Ursprung des deutschen Trauerspiels* (1928), *Gesammelte Schriften*, vol. 1, 359.

13. *Ursprung des deutschen Trauerspiels*, 310; quoted verbatim from the earlier "Schicksal und Charakter," 173.

14. *Ursprung des deutschen Trauerspiels*, 318–19.

15. "Trauer und Melancholie," 199 f.

16. "Trauer und Melancholie," 209.

17. See Paul de Man, "The Rhetoric of Temporality" (1969), *Blindness and Insight*, 2nd ed. (Minneapolis: University of Minnesota Press, 1982), 187–228, responding to Jean Starobinski, "Ironie und Melancholie," *Der Monat* 18 (1966): 22–35; also my further discussion in "Allegorie, Ironie und Wiederholung," *Poetik und Hermeneutik*, vol. 9 (1981), 561–565.

18. Thus, for example, Helm Stierlin, *Das Tun des Einen ist das Tun des Anderen* (Frankfurt: Suhrkamp, 1971), 72.

19. Sandor Ferenczi, "Zur Begriffsbestimmung der Introjektion" (1912), *Schriften zur Psychoanalyse,* vol. 1 (Frankfurt: Fischer, 1970), 100–102. Cf. Karl Abraham, "Versuch einer Entwicklungsgeschichte der Libido auf Grund der Psychoanalyse seelischer Störungen" (1924), *Psychoanalytische Studien,* vol. 1 (Frankfurt: Fischer, 1969), 135.

20. See, for example, Jean-Baptiste Pontalis, *Apres Freud* (Paris: Seuil, 1965), 167 f.

21. Cf. Jacques Derrida, *Limited, Inc.* (1977), new edition (Evanston: Northwestern University Press, 1988).

22. Maria Torok, "Maladie du deuil et fantasme du cadavre exquis" (1968); rprt. in Nicolas Abraham, *L'écorce et le noyau* (*Anasémies* 2) (Paris: Aubier-Flammarion, 1978), 237–38.

23. "Trauer und Melancholie," 209; and in the following 210–11. *Tr.* The translation follows here, with modifications, Joan Riviere's version in *General Psychological Theory,* ed. Philip Rieff (New York: Collier, 1963), 176.

24. *Memoires for Paul de Man,* trans. Cecile Lindsay, Jonathan Culler, and Eduardo Cadava (New York: Columbia University Press, 1986), 6, 21, and 32.

25. Jacques Derrida, "FORS," introduction, *Cryptonymie: Le verbier de l'Homme aux loups* (*Anasémies* 1), by Nicolas Abraham and Maria Torok (Paris: Aubier-Flammarion, 1976), 17.

26. "FORS: The Anglish Words of Nicolas Abraham and Maria Torok," trans. Barbara Johnson, *Georgia Review* 31 (Spring 1977): 64–116; rprt. in Abraham and Torok, *The Wolfman's Magic Word,* ed. Nicholas Rand (Minneapolis: Minnesota University Press, 1986), xi–xii (translator's note).

27. Walter Benjamin, "Zentralpark," *Gesammelte Schriften,* vol. 1, 681 (fragment 32a). Cf. Norbert Elias, *Über den Prozeß der Zivilisation* (Basel: Haus zum Falken, 1939/Bern: Francke, 1969), vol. 1, lxii–iii; vol. 2, 409.

28. See, for example, Avital Ronell, *Dictations—On Haunted Writing* (Bloomington: Indiana University Press, 1986); Lawrence Rickels, *Aberrations of Mourning* (Detroit: 1988); Nicholas Rand, *Le cryptage et la vie des oeuvres* (Paris: Aubier, 1989).

29. See Nicolas Abraham and Maria Torok, "De la topique rélitaire—Notations sur une métapsychologie du secret," *L'écorce et le noyau,* 252–257. For the hermetic tradition, cf. Heinrich Rombach, *Welt und Gegenwelt* (Basel: Herder, 1983).

30. Joachim Küchenhoff and Peter Warsitz, "Die Spur des ganz Anderen—Freuds Nosographie und der psychotische Text am Beispiel Hölderlins," *Fragmente* 17–18 (1985): 212.

31. *Ursprung des deutschen Trauerspiels,* 318, and above 406; cf. "Zentralpark" 689 (fragment 44). For my treatment of Benjamin, see Bettine Menke, *Figuren des Umwegs—Benjamins Sprachphilosophie,* diss. phil., University of Konstanz, 1986, published as *Sprachfiguren: Name-Allegorie-Bild nach Walter Benjamin* (Munich: Fink, 1991).

32. Jacques Derrida, "Speculer sur Freud," *La carte postale de Socrate à Freud et au-delà* (Paris: Galilée, 1980), 356; trans. Alan Bass (Chicago: Chicago University Press, 1987), 335. See my "Kaleidoscope of Mourning," *Pequod* 35 (1993), 13–23: 17.

33. Derrida's paraphrase, "FORS," 57; and below, Abraham and Torok, *Cryptonymie,* 231.

34. Emanuel Levinas, "Die Spur des Anderen" (1947), *Die Spur des Anderen,* trans. and ed. Wolfgang Nikolaus Krewani (Freiburg: Rombach, 1983), 231 ff; trans. Alphonso Lingis, "The Trace of the Other," *Deconstruction in Context,* ed. Mark Taylor (Chicago: Chicago University Press, 1986), 345–359.

35. Nicolas Abraham and Maria Torok, "Deuil *ou* mélancholie: Introjecter-incorper" (1972), *L'écorce et le noyau,* 261 (their emphasis).

36. See the famous phrase, *Ursprung des deutschen Trauerspiels,* 351.

37. See, for example, Roy Schafter, *A New Language for Psychoanalysis* (New Haven: Yale University Press, 1985), 333, 354.

38. *Cryptonymie,* 232 (italics: German in the original).

39. Derrida, "FORS," 24; as well as Abraham and Torok, *Cryptonymie,* 232/33.

40. Hans Blumenberg, *Arbeit am Mythos* (Frankfurt: Suhrkamp, 1979), 689 (last page, last line).

I. Silva—Impossible Ode (Haller and Kant)

1. *Tr.* With the aim of providing a poem in English, I have tried, wherever possible, to follow Haller's original meter and rhyme. In cases, however, where a rhyme in English would require the introduction of new vocabulary, I have chosen instead to follow the literal sense of the line.

2. Odo Marquard, "Der angeklagte und der entlastete Mensch" (1980), *Abschied vom Prinzipiellen* (Stuttgart: Reclam, 1981), 46; below 53.

3. Leif Ludwig Albertsen, *Das Lehrgedicht—Eine Geschichte der antikisierenden Sachepik in der neueren deutschen Literatur* (Aarhus: University Press, 1967), 236.

4. Karl Richter, *Literatur und Naturwissenschaft—Eine Studie zur Lyrik der Aufklärung* (Munich: Fink, 1972), 108 ff.

5. See the classical instance of Paul Böckmann, *Formgeschichte der deutschen Dichtung*, vol. 1 (Hamburg: Hoffmann and Campe, 1949), 628 ff.

6. Hans Magnus Enzensberger, *Mausoleum: Siebenunddreißig Balladen aus der Geschichte des Fortschritts* (Frankfurt: Suhrkamp, 1975), 39.

7. Johann Zimmermann, *Das Leben des Herrn von Haller* (Zürich: Orell and Füssli, 1755), 100.

8. *Über die Einsamkeit*, vol. 2 (Frankfurt and Leipzig, 1785) 176; quoted in Hans-Jürgen Schings, *Melancholie und Aufklärung: Melancholiker und ihre Kritiker in Erfahrungsseelenkunde und Literatur des 18. Jarhhunderts* (Stuttgart: Metzler, 1977), 139.

9. Hans Blumenberg, *Lebenszeit und Weltzeit* (Frankfurt: Suhrkamp, 1986), 213 (Excursus: "On the missing history of immortality").

10. Immanuel Kant, *Kritik der reinen Vernunft*, A 613. For a commentary on this passage, see Heinz Heimsoeth, *Transzendentale Dialektik: Ein Kommentar zu Kants Kritik der reinen Vernunft*, vol. 3 (Berlin: de Gruyter, 1966–71), 501 and 146n.

11. Odo Marquard, *Skeptische Methode im Blick auf Kant* (Freiburg und Munich: Alber, 1958), 38 f. See in particular Martin Heidegger, *Kant und das Problem der Metaphysik* (1929), 2nd ed. (Frankfurt: Klostermann, 1951), e. g. 147 (para. 31).

12. Eduard Stäuble, "Albrecht von Haller, der Dichter zwischen den Zeiten—Versuch einer stilkritischen und geistesgeschichtlichen Interpretation seines *Unvollkommenen Gedichts über die Ewigkeit*," *Der Deutschunterricht* 8 (1956): 9

13. Anna Ischer, *Albrecht v. Haller und das klassische Altertum* (Bern: Haupt, 1928), 64.

14. See in particular Johann Jacob Breitinger, *Kritische Dichtkunst* (Zurich: Orell, 1740), vol. 2, 356 (chapter on "heart-moving writing").

15. Here, and in the following, I draw upon Konrad Krautter, *Die Renaissance der Bukolik in der lateinischen Literatur des XIV. Jahrhunderts: von Dante bis Petrarca* (Munich: Fink, 1983), 109 ff. , esp. 155 f.

16. Johann Georg Zimmermann, *Das Leben des Herrn von Haller*, 83. Cf. Elschenbroich's anthology, which accurately assesses the older editions (Hirzel, Frey), *Die Alpen und andere Gedichte* (Stuttgart: Reclam, 1965), 75.

17. Again Krautter, *Die Renaissance der Bukolik*, 122. Cf. Hans Jörg Spitz, *Die Metaphorik des geistigen Schriftsinns* (Munich: Fink, 1972), 130 ff.

18. See Ferdinand Hauenthal, ed. (1856) (under *Carmina* I, 24, *nefas*). Most recently Michael C. F. Putnam, "The Languages of Horace Odes I. 24," *Classical Journal* 88 (1993), 123–135: 131.

19. Krautter, *Die Renaissance der Bukolik*, 122.

20. Benjamin, *Ursprung des deutschen Trauerspiels* (1928), *Gesammelten Schriften*, vol. 1 (Frankfurt: Suhrkamp, 1974), 406.

21. See Karl S. Guthke, "Hallers Unvollkommene Ode über die Ewigkeit: Veranlassung und Entstehung," *Deutsche Vierteljahrsshrift* 48 (1974), 528–545: 534.

22. Anselm Haverkamp, "Saving the Subject—Randbemerkungen zur Veränderung der Lyrik," *Poetica* 14 (1982), 70–91: 75 ff.

23. *Ursprung des deutschen Trauerspiels*, 246; below 329, 318. See the more general description by Karsten Harries, *The Bavarian Rococo Church: Between Faith and Aestheticism* (New Haven: Yale University Press, 1983), 201 ff.

24. Benjamin, "Zentralpark," *Gesammelte Schriften*, vol. 1, 689 (fragment 44).

25. The remark appears in an unedited letter quoted by Guthke, "Hallers *Unvollkommene Ode*," 539 (Werlhof's emphasis).

26. Instead of Hirzel's edition I prefer the just as reliable collection by Adolf Frey (ed.), *Haller und Salis-Seewis* (Berlin, Stuttgart: Spemann, 1893), 115 ff. "Trauerode, beim Absterben seiner geliebten Mariane"; and below, 60 f. "Doris."

27. "Über naive und sentimentalische Dichtung," *Schillers Werke* (Nationalausgabe), vol. 20, ed. Benno von Wiese (Weimar: Böhlau, 1962), 455.

28. Friedrich Rudolph Ludwig Freiherr von Canitz, *Gedichte*, ed. Jürgen Stenzel (Tübingen: Niemeyer, 1982), 327. See Ischer, *Haller*, 203.

29. See Paul de Man, "Semiology and Rhetoric" (1973), *Allegories of Reading* (New Haven: Yale University Press, 1979), 9.

30. Sigmund Freud, "Trauer und Melancholie" (1917), *Studienausgabe*, vol. 3 (Frankfurt: Suhrkamp, 1975), 201, 203.

31. William Empson, *Seven Types of Ambiguity*, rev. ed. (New York: New Directions, 1947), 192.

32. *Tr.* See Anselm Haverkamp, "Fest/Schrift: Festschreibung unbeschreiblicher Feste in Klopstocks Ode," *Poetik und Hermeneutik*, vol. 14 (1989), 276–298.

33. Eduard Stäuble, *Albrecht von Haller "Über den Ursprung des Übels"* (Zürich: Atlantis, 1959), 152.

34. *Tr.* As can be seen from the double usage, *Reiz* in German means both "charm" and, as in the *Reiz/Reaktion* schema, "stimulus."

II. By The Figtree—Mnemosyne (Hölderlin and Hegel)

1. Friedrich Beissner, "Hölderlin's letzte Hymne" (1948), *Hölderlin—Reden und Aufsätze*, 2nd ed. (Köln/Wien: Böhlau, 1969),

211–46; quoted in the "Erläuterungen" of the *Grosse Stuttgarter Ausgabe*, vol. 2: 830, commentary for Mnemosyne, ll. 50–51.

2. *Frankfurter Ausgabe*, ed. Dietrich E. Sattler: *Einleitung* (Frankfurt: Roter Stern, 1975), commentary for ll. 52, 69.

3. Flemming Roland-Jensen, "Hölderlin's *Mnemosyne*," *ZfdPh* 98 (1979): 237. For an opposing view, see the polemical essay by Walter Hof, "*Mnemosyne* und die Interpretation der letzten hymnischen Versuche Hölderlins," *GRM* NF 32 (1982): 420.

4. Bernhard Böschenstein, *Konkordanz zu Hölderlins Gedichten nach 1800* (Göttlingen: Vandenhoeck und Rupprecht, 1964), 27.

5. Cf. Rolf Zuberbühler, *Hölderlins Erneuerung der Sprache aus ihren etymologischen Ursprüngen* (Berlin: Erich Schmidt, 1960).

6. Sigmund Freud, "Trauer und Melancholie" (1917), *Studienausgabe*, vol. 3 (Frankfurt: Fischer, 1975), 203.

7. See, in addition to Beissner's "Erläuterungen," Jochen Schmidt, *Hölderlins letzte Hymnen: "Andenken" und "Mnemosyne"* (Tübingen: Niemeyer, 1970), 59–70.

8. Cf. William Bedell Standord, ed., *Sophocles's Ajax* (London: Macmillan, 1963), 275.

9. See in particular Schmidt, *Hölderlins letzte Hymnen*, 63.

10. Peter Szondi, *Hölderlin-Studien* (Frankfurt: Suhrkamp, 1967), 146.

11. Theodor W. Adorno, "Parataxis—Zur späten Lyrik Hölderlins" (1964), *Gesammelte Schriften*, vol. 11 (Frankfurt: Suhrkamp, 1974), 477 ff.

12. Walter Benjamin, "Zwei Gedichte von Friedrich Hölderlin" (1920), *Gesammelte Schriften*, vol. 2 (Frankfurt: Suhrkamp, 1974), 112. Tr. Note the translation into and confrontation with the structuralist lexicon throughout this stage of the analysis.

13. See already the commentary by Friedrich August Wolf, ed., *Theogonia Hesiodea* (Halle: Ioh. Iac. Gebauer, 1783), 70.

14. Benjamin, *Ursprung des deutschen Trauerspiels* (1928), *Gesammelte Schriften*, vol. 1 (Frankfurt: Suhrkamp, 1974), 353. See

Theodor W. Adorno, "Die Idee der Naturgeschichte" (1932), *Gesammelte Schriften*, vol. 1 (Frankfurt: Suhrkamp, 1972), 357.

15. "Über den Unterschied der Dichtarten," *Sämtliche Werke* (Grosse Stuttgarter Ausgabe), vol. 4, 266; as quoted by Szondi, *Hölderlin-Studien*, 119; see 158.

16. Paul de Man, *Allegories of Reading* (New Haven: Yale University Press, 1979), 205. See Carol Jacobs, "Allegories of Reading Paul de Man," *Reading de Man Reading*, ed. Lindsay Waters, Wlad Godzich (Minneapolis: University of Minnesota Press, 1989), 115.

17. For more on the terminological translations of more recent theories of metaphor, see Ivor Armstrong Richards, *Philosophy of Rhetoric* (New York: Oxford University Press), chapters 5 and 6.

18. Theodor W. Adorno, *Äesthetische Theorie, Gesammelte Schriften*, vol. 7 (Frankfurt: Suhrkamp, 1970), 202.

19. *Dido*, in *Schillers Werke* (Nationalausgabe), vol. 2, ed. Norbert Oellers (Weimar: Böhlau, 1983), 59 (l. 1023).

20. William Empson, *Seven Types of Ambiguity*, rev. ed. (New York: New Directions, 1947), 214.

21. Cf. Karl Vietor, *Geschichte der deutschen Ode* (Munich: Drei Masken, 1923), 145 ff.

22. Paul de Man, "Anthropomorphism and Trope in the Lyric," *The Rhetoric of Romanticism* (New York: Columbia University Press, 1984), 261.

23. Paul de Man, "The Image of Rousseau in the Poetry of Hölderlin" (1965), *The Rhetoric of Romanticism*, 45.

24. As quoted by Bernhard Böschenstein, *Hölderlins Rheinhymne*, 2nd ed. (Zürich: Atlantis, 1968), 91. See Jean Starobinski, *La transparence et l'obstacle* (Paris: Gallimard, 1957, 1971), 310–315.

25. Jean-Jacques Rousseau, *Les rêveries du promeneur solitaire* (1782), *Oeuvres complètes*, vol. 1, ed. Marcel Raymond (Paris: Gallimard, 1959), 1040.

26. Walter Benjamin, "Zentralpark," *Gesammelte Schriften*, vol. 1, 676 (fragment 28).

27. Reinhard Meyer-Kalkus, "Mnemosyne," *Historisches Wörterbuch der Philosophie*, ed. Joachim Ritter et al. (Basel: Schwabe, 1971–84), 1442.

28. Dieter Henrich, *Hegel im Kontext* (Frankfurt: Suhrkamp, 1971), 34.

29. Georg Wilhelm Friedrich Hegel, *Phänomenologie des Geistes* (Philosophische Bibliothek), ed. Johannes Hoffmeister, 6th ed. (Hamburg: Meiner, 1952), 564.

30. "Anthropomorphism and Trope in the Lyric," 247.

31. "Anthropomorphism and Trope in the Lyric," 247.

32. "Parataxis," 485. Cf. Paul de Man, "Keats and Hölderlin," *Comparative Literature* 8 (1956): 44.

33. Paul de Man, "Foreword," *Dissimulating Harmony*, by Carol Jacobs (Baltimore: Johns Hopkins University Press, 1978), xi.

34. "Anmerkungen zum Oedipus," *Sämtliche Werke* (Grosse Stuttgarter Ausgabe), vol. 5, 201; as quoted by Jochen Schmidt, "Der Begriff des Zorns in Hölderlins Spätwerk," *Hölderlin Jahrbuch* 15 (1967–68): 157.

35. See Barbara Vinken, "Encore: Francesca da Rimini," *Deutsche Vierteljahrsschrift* 62 (1988), 395–415.

36. Gregory Nagy, *The Best of the Achaeans* (Baltimore: Johns Hopkins University Press, 1979), 31; see also chapters 2 and 6.

37. For the larger sweep of this motif, see Jean Starobinski, *Trois fureurs* (Paris: Gallimard, 1975), 78 ff.

38. "Aus dem Ajax des Sophokles," *Sämtliche Werke* (Grosse Stuttgarter Ausgabe), vol. 5, *Ajax*, 279 (ll. 596–645).

39. Helm Stierlin, "Creativity and Schizophrenic Psychosis in Hölderlin's Fate," *Hölderlin—An Early Modern*, ed. Emory E. George (Ann Arbor: University of Michigan Press, 1972), 215.

40. *Seven Types of Ambiguity*, 192. Cf. Paul de Man, "The Dead End of Formalist Criticism" (1956), *Blindness and Insight: Essays in the Rhetoric of Contemporary Criticism*, 2nd ed. (1972; Minneapolis: Minnesota University Press, 1983), 237.

41. "Zentralpark," 589 (fragment 44).

42. Dietrich E. Sattler, *Friedrich Hölderlin—144 Fliegende Briefe*, vol. 2 (Darmstadt/Neuwied: Luchterhand, 1981), 610 (letter 131); cf. vol. 1, 103–5 (letter 20).

43. Jacques Derrida, "FORS," introduction, *Cryptonymie—Le verbier de l'Homme aux loups*, by Nicolas Abraham and Maria Torok (Paris: Aubier-Flammarion, 1976), 26.

44. Rolf Zuberbühler, *Hölderlins Erneuerung der Sprache aus ihrem etymologischen Ursprüngen* (Berlin: Erich Schmidt, 1960), 108.

45. See de Man, "Anthropomorphism and Trope," 248.

46. *Lesmosyne*: M. L. West, ed., Hesiod *Theogony* (Oxford: Clarendon Press, 1966), 175, 55n.

III. Secluded Laurel—Andenken (Hölderlin and Heidegger)

1. Friedrich Beissner, ed. , *Große Stuttgarter Ausgabe*, vol. 2/II (Stuttgart: Kohlhammer, 1952), Erläuterungen, 802.

2. Dieter Henrich, *Der Gang des Andenkens—Beobachtungen und Gedanken zu Hölderlins Gedicht* (Stuttgart: Klett-Cotta, 1986), 185.

3. Paul de Man, "Les exégèses de Hölderlin par Martin Heidegger," *Critique* 100/101 (1955): 809 (the whole sentence is underscored); trans. in *Blindness and Insight: Essays in the Rhetoric of Contemporary Criticism* (Minneapolis: University Press of Minnesota, 1983), 254.

4. Paul de Man, *The Rhetoric of Romanticism* (New York: Columbia University Press, 1984), vi (with reference to Adorno's parataxis essay).

5. See Paul H. Fry, "Non-Construction: History, Structure, and the Occasion of the Literary," *The Yale Journal of Criticism* 1/2 (1988): 45–64.

6. See Hauke Brunkhorst's chapter on Adorno's Hölderlin in his *Dialektik der Moderne* (Munich: Piper, 1990), 200, 204. It is impor-

tant to observe that de Man's reading of Hölderlin is no more Heideggerian than Adorno's.

7. The anamnesis passage from "Parataxis," *Noten zur Literatur, Gesammelte Schriften*, vol. 11 (Frankfurt: Suhrkamp, 1974), 482 ff. , 466.

8. Martin Heidegger, "Wie wenn am Feiertage . . . " (1939), *Erläuterungen zu Hölderlins Dichtung, Gesamtausgabe*, vol. 4 (Frankfurt: Klostermann, 1982), 55.

9. Martin Heidegger, *Hölderlin und das Wesen der Dichtung*, 1st and 2nd eds. (Munich: Langen/Müller, 1937), on the left endpaper. The wording corresponds to that of the edition of Hellingrath's writings, *Hölderlin-Vermächtnis*, ed. Ludwig von Pigenot (Munich, 1936), 2nd enlarged ed. 1944, and its foreword, 9.

10. See Alexander and Margarete Mitscherlich, *Die Unfähigkeit zu trauern* (Munich: Piper, 1967).

11. Henrich, *Der Gang des Andenkens*, 190.

12. Heidegger, *Erläuterungen zu Hölderlins Dichtung*, 42.

13. Cyrus Hamlin, "The Poetics of Remembrance," ts. 2; trans. "Die Poetik des Gedächtnisses," *Hölderlin-Jahrbuch* 24 (1984/85): 120.

14. Quoted and commented on by Odo Marquard, "Felix culpa?" *Poetik und Hermeneutik*, vol. 9 (1981): 68. The following quotation from Erich Fried comes from a volume of his poetry, *Die Freiheit den Mund aufzumachen* (Berlin: Wagenbach, 1972), 26.

15. Cf. Bernhard Lypp, "Mein ist die Rede vom Vaterland: Heidegger und Hölderlin," *Merkur* 41, No 456 (1987): 122. In reaction to the present study, see Lypp's "Hölderlins Mnemosyne," *Das Rätsel der Zeit*, ed. Hans Michael Baumgartner (Freiburg: Alber, 1993), 291–330.

16. Wolfgang Binder, "Hölderlin: Andenken," *Turm-Vorträge* 1985–86, ed. Uvo Hölscher (Tübingen: Hölderlin-Gesellschaft, 1986), 13.

17. See, meanwhile, Dieter Henrich, *Der Grund im Bewußtsein: Untersuchungen zu Hölderlins Denken (1794–1795)* (Stuttgart: Klett-Cotta, 1992).

18. Martin Heidegger, *Hölderlins Hymne Andenken* (Frankfurt: Klostermann, 1982), 54–55.

19. For the "nobility" of this picture ("a noble pair"), see Hans Jonas, "The Nobility of Sight," *Philosophy and Phenomenology Research* 14 (1953/54): 507–519.

20. Henrich, *Gang des Andenkens*, 92–93. For a more detailed account, see Bernhard Böschenstein, *Frucht des Gewitters—Hölderlins Dionysos als Gott der Revolution* (Frankfurt: Insel, 1989), 71, 187 ff.

21. de Man, "Les exégèses de Hölderlin par Martin Heidegger," 809, 810, 812 (Chadwick's translation).

22. On the dialectic of "tenor" and "vehicle," see again I. A. Richards, *The Philosophy of Rhetoric* (New York, 1936).

23. I refer here only to the genealogy of motives of the aesthetic discovery of landscape in Petrarch: from Jacob Burckhardt through Ernst Cassirer and Joachim Ritter to Hans Blumenberg and Hans Robert Jauss. See Karlheinz Stierle, *Petrarcas Landschaften* (publications and lectures of the Petrarca-Institut Cologne) (Krefeld, 1979), 52–67. In this regard, contrast the example from Rousseau's *Nouvelle Héloise* in Paul de Man, "The Rhetoric of Temporality" (1969), in *Blindness and Insight*, 208.

24. Jean Pierre Lefebvre, "Auch die Stege sind Holzwege," *Hölderlin vu de France*, ed. Bernhard Böschenstein and Jacques le Rider (Tübingen: Narr, 1987), 64.

25. See Pierre Courcelle, *Recherches sur les Confessions de Saint Augustin* (1950), new ed. (Paris, 1968), 193, n2 (with parallel citations). As Courcelle's subtitle "Literary Fiction and Reality" shows, the passage has always been crucial for this question. Cf. Henri Irénée Marrou, "La Querelle autour du *Tolle, lege*," *Revue d'Histoire Ecclesiastique* 53 (1958), 52; and the detailed notes in the edition of Bibliothèque Augustinienne, *Oeuvres de Saint Augustin* XIV, ed. A. Solignac (Paris, 1962), 546–549.

26. John Freccero, "The Figtree and the Laurel—Petrarch's Poetics" (1975), in *Literary Theory/Renaissance Texts*, ed. Patricia Parker and David Quint (Baltimore: Johns Hopkins University Press, 1986), 24 ff.

27. See Rolf Zuberbühler, *Hölderlins Erneuerung der Sprache aus ihren etymologischen Ursprüngen* (Berlin: Erich Schmidt, 1969), 109.

28. In Rousseau's *Confessions*, the famous "illumination on the road to Vincennes" (Chapter VIII) takes place first under a tree (in the manuscript), then definitively "sous un Chêne": *Oeuvres complètes* I, ed. Bernhard Gagnebin and Marcel Raymond (Paris: Gallimard, 1959), 351 with footnote (a) 1427. This is no uncharacteristic variation on Augustine for which there are parallels; see, for example, the return of Augustine's stolen pears in the stolen apples of Rousseau, displacements that obviously are not arbitrary. And by the way, also the oak was already a laurel: see Ernest H. Wilkins, "The Coronation of Petrarch" (1943), in *The Making of the Canzoniere and other Petrarchan Studies* (Roma: Ed. Storia e Letteratura, 1951), 16.

29. The postscript brings together answers to the encouragements and objections this paper has elicted from Dieter Henrich, Paul Fry, Reinhart Herzog, Wolfgang Iser, and Paul Ricoeur in conferences at Yale, Cerisy-la-Salle, and Konstanz.

30. "Gemeinsame Interpretation von Apollinaires *Arbre*," chair Hans Robert Jauß, *Poetik und Hermeneutik*, vol. 2 (1966), 472. The notion of 'momentary evidence' taken up by Dieter Henrich in this debate had been introduced by Hans Blumenberg, "Wirklichkeitsbegriff und Möglichkeit des Romans," *Poetik und Hermeneutik*, vol. 1 (1964), 1–27.

31. Cf. the Heideggerian Hermann Gundert, "Enthusiasmos und Logos bei Plato," *Lexis* II (1949), fasc. 1: 45.

32. Wolfgang Iser, "Figurationen des lyrischen Subjekts," *Poetik und Hermeneutik*, vol. 8 (1979), 748.

33. *Husserliana* XXIII, 392; cited in Eckhard Lobsien, *Landschaft in Texten* (Stuttgart: Metzler, 1981), 96. An underestimated commonplace also in the criticism of Henrich by Renate Homann, "Das Besondere und das Allgemeine in der Dichtung" (review of *Der Gang des Andekens*), *Zeitschrift für philosophische Forschung* 42 (1988): 642.

34. See the literary survey by Hans Peter Duerr, *Traumzeit— Über die Grenze zwischen Wildnis und Zivilisation* (Frankfurt, 1978), 206, n37.

35. One could compare the—in part questionable—study by Konrad Burdach, *Der Gral* (Stuttgart, 1938), 37 ff.

36. See—with a view especially to Heidegger's reading— Jacques Derrida, "Comment ne pas parler—Dénegations," *Psyché— Inventions de l'autre* (Paris: Galilée, 1987), 588 ff.

37. Martin Heidegger, "Andenken" (1943), *Erläuterungen zu Hölderlins Dichtung*, 151, last paragraph.

38. See Paul de Man, "Tropes (Rilke)" (1972), *Allegories of Reading* (New Haven: Yale University Press, 1979), 50.

39. Anselm Haverkamp, "Laura's Metamorphosen—Deconstruction einer lyrischen Figur in der Prosa der *Maulwürfe,*" *Deutsche Vierteljahrsschrift* 58 (1984): 343 f.

40. Cf. Kenneth Cool, "The Petrarchan Landscape as Palimpsest," *Journal of Medieval and Renaissance Studies* 11 (1981): 89 f. , 94 f.

41. Leonard Forster, *The Icy Fire* (Cambridge, England, 1969), chapter 2 and "Tail Piece."

IV. Wild Elder—The Churchyard (Hölderlin and Kant)

1. Wilhelm Waiblinger, *Friedrich Hölderlins Leben, Dichtung und Wahnsinn* (Leipzig, 1831), quoted from *Frankfurter Ausgabe,* vol. 9 (Darmstadt/Neuwied: Luchterhand, 1984), 157.

2. *Zum ewigen Frieden—Ein philosophischer Entwurf* (Königsberg, 1795), 3.

3. Kant had earlier experienced the relationship of such reasoning to this brand of hospitality in the gift of some "Dutch herring," which one of his skeptical admirers, concerned about his worldly well-being, had sent him together with a request for further explanation of the 'metaphysical ideas' of God, soul, and immortality. See H. Y. Groenewegen, "Der erste Kampf um Kant in Holland," *Kant-Studien* 29 (1924): 307.

4. Tr. 'Post–figural' according to Albrecht Schöne, *Emblematik und Drama im Zeitalter des Barock* (Munich: Beck, 1964).

5. See Hans Blumenberg, *Paradigmen zu einer Metaphorologie* (Bonn: Bouvier, 1960).

6. D. E. Sattler, "*as rovescio*: Hölderlin nach 1806," *Le pauvre Holterling* 7 (1984): 26 f. , 28.

7. Theodor W. Adorno, *Negative Dialektik* (Frankfurt: Suhrkamp, 1966), 376. Beethoven's "Great symphony, with its solo and choral arrangement of Schiller's song to joy introduced in the finale," was originally performed in Vienna on May 7, 1824; the composition of the ode dates from Beethoven's Bonn period (around 1792). Schiller's first version appeared in the second volume of *Thalia* in 1786.

8. For the strategy of the whole poem, Bart Philipsen, "De *arme* Hölderlin en de politiek van de dwaasheid," *Pi—Tijdschrift voor Poezie* 6, No. 4 (1987): 51 ff. ; "*Mit Untertänigkeit Scardanelli*—Toenadering tot de 'Idylle' van Hölderlins laatste Gedichten," *Restant* 15 (1987): 199 ff.

9. Cf. Rainer Nägele, *Text, Geschichte und Subjektivität in Hölderlins Dichtung—"Uneßbarer Schrift gleich"* (Stuttgart: Metzler, 1985), 108 (on "humoristic constellation").

10. Walter Benjamin, "Zwei Gedichte von Friedrich Hölderlin" (1914), *Gesammelte Schriften*, vol. 2 (Frankfurt: Suhrkamp, 1974), 126, 117. *Blödigkeit* occurs in the volume *Oden* of the Frankfurt edition, vol. 2, 320 (reworked lines 1–8).

11. "Der späte Hölderlin" (1936), *Eugen Gottlob Winkler*, ed. Walter Jens (Frankfurt: Fischer, 1960), 152, 145.

12. Erasmus von Rotterdam, *Encomium moriae* (1509), trans. *In Praise of Folly*.

13. Peter Szondi, *Einführung in die literarische Hermeneutik* (Studienausgabe der Vorlesungen V) (Frankfurt: Suhrkamp, 1975), 197 f.

14. Rainer Nägele, "Friedrich Hölderlin: Die F(V)erse des Achilles," *Fragment und Totalität*, ed. Lucien Dällenbach and Christiaan L. Hart Nibbrig (Frankfurt: Suhrkamp, 1984), 206.

15. In particular in the report from Roman Jakobson and Grete Lübbe-Groethues, "Ein Blick auf *Die Aussicht* von Hölderlin," in Jakobson's collection *Hölderlin, Klee, Brecht—Zur Wortkunst dreier Gedichte*, ed. Elmar Holenstein (Frankfurt: Suhrkamp, 1976).

16. See, in the wake of Dilthey and Husserl, Moritz Geiger, *Fragment über den Begriff des Unbewußten und die psychische Realität. Jahrbuch für Philosophie und phänomenologische Forschung*, vol. 4 (Halle: Niemeyer, 1921), 15ff. Geiger is known for his groundbreaking *Phänomenologie des ästhetischen Genusses*, first to appear in the same *Jahrbuch*, vol. 1 (Halle: Niemeyer, 1913).

17. Pierre Bertaux, *Hölderlin-Variationen* (Frankfurt: Suhrkamp, 1984), 2 (last version of the well-known thesis).

18. Michael Franz, "Annäherung an Hölderlins Verücktheit," *Hölderlin-Jahrbuch* 22 (1981/82): 285 ff.

19. Jean Laplanche, *Hölderlin et la question du père* (Paris: PUF, 1961).

20. Quoted in the commentary of the Frankfurt edition, vol. 9, 50.

21. *Ursprung des deutschen Trauerspiels*, 405 f.

22. Cf. Andrzej Warminski, "*Patmos*: The Senses of Interpretation" (1976), *Readings in Interpretation—Hölderlin, Hegel, Heidegger* (Minneapolis: University of Minnesota Press, 1987), 80 ff.

23. See Bernhard Böschenstein, "Hölderlins späteste Gedichte," *Hölderlin-Jahrbuch* 14 (1965/66): 55.

24. See Anselm Haverkamp, "Fest/Schrift: Festschreibung unbeschreiblicher Feste in Klopstocks *Ode von der Fahrt auf der Zürchersee*," *Poetik und Hermeneutik*, vol. 9 (Munich: Fink, 1989), 285.

25. D. E. Sattler, *Friedrich Hölderlin—144 fliegende Briefe*, vol. 1 (Darmstadt-Neuwied: Luchterhand, 1981), 74.

26. *An Thills Grab* as well as *Die Meinige[n]* and other adolescent poems follow the Große Stuttgarter edition, vol. 1, 83–84; 15–20. (The first volume of the Frankfurter edition has still not appeared.)

27. Cf. in detail Volker Schäfer, "Vom *fackelschimmer . . . auf des Theuren Sarg* bis zu *Seiner heiligkeit Herrn Teuffel*—Überlieferungssplitter zu Friedrich Hölderlin," *Hölderlin-Jahrbuch* 26 (1988/89): 402 f.

28. *Hölderlin et la question du père*, 86.

29. After the Große Stuttgarter edition, vol. 6, 333 (nr. 180); Laplanche's commentary, *Hölderlin et la question du père*, 86–88.

30. *Hölderlin et la question du père*, 88.

31. Cf. Sattler's conjectures on the keyword "Holunder," *Friedrich Hölderlin—144 fliegende Briefe*, vol. 1, 75. In addition, Bart Philipsen, "*En less mij, o gij bloesems van Duitsland*: Hölderlins late Hymnen," *In het licht van de letter—Zes oefeningen in deconstructie*, Herman Servotte, Ludo Verbeeck and Dirk De Schutter, eds. (Leuven: Peeters, 1988), 86 f.

32. "Le *non* du père" (review article on Laplanche's *Hölderlin et la question du père*), *Critique* 178 (1962), 195.

33. Joel Dor, *Introduction à la lecture de Lacan*, vol. 1 (Paris: Denoel, 1985), 126. See there his summary of pertinent passages, including unpublished seminars, here especially from *Les formations de l'inconscient* (1957–58).

34. Cf. Jacques Derrida's critique with respect to Artaud, "La parole soufflée" (1965), *L'Ecriture et la difference* (Paris: Minuit, 1967), 356 ff.

35. *Hölderlin et la question du père*, 44.

36. Jacques Lacan, "D'une question préliminaire à tout traitement possible de la psychose" (1959), *Écrits* (Paris: Seuil, 1966), 575 and "Postscriptum," 579 f.

37. Cf. Guy Rosalato, "Du Père" (1966), *Essais sur le symbolique* (Paris: Gallimard, 1969), 45 ff.

38. "D'une question préliminaire," 577.

39. *Hölderlin et la question du père*, 47.

40. Paul Ricoeur, *La métaphore vive* (Paris: Seuil, 1975), 361. See the commentary by Jean Greisch, "Les mots et les roses—La Métaphore chez Martin Heidegger," *Revue des sciences philosophique et théologiques* 57 (1973): 443–453. Tr. The English translation of *La métaphore vive* as *The Rule of Metaphor*, trans. Robert Czerny (London: Routledge and Kegan Paul, 1978), misses the entire point.

41. See Jacques Derrida, "Mythologie blanche—La métaphore dans le texte philosophique" (1971), *Marges—De la philosophie* (Paris: Minuit, 1972), 307.

42. Ludo Verbeeck, "Récit mythique ou appel transgressiv? A propos du poème *Der Winkel von Hardt* de Friedrich Hölderlin,"

Mélanges de linguistique et de littérature, offerts au Henri Draye, ed. Jacques Lerot and Rudolf Kern (Louvain: Nauwelaerts, 1978), 234, 238.

43. "Hölderlins späteste Gedichte," 43.

Mourning Becomes Melancholia: Ode on Melancholy (Keats and Locke)

1. John Keats, "Ode on Melancholy," *The Poems of John Keats,* ed. Miriam Allott (London: Longman, 1970), 539, ll. 6–7; hereafter cited in text by line number.

2. Sigmund Freud, "Trauer und Melancholie" (1917) and "Jenseits des Lustprincips" (1921), *Studienausgabe,* vol. 3 (Frankfurt: Fischer, 1975), 193–212, 213–72. See Jacques Derrida, *La carte postale de Socrate á Freud et au-delá* (Paris: Galilée, 1980), 277 ff. , 341 ff.

3. Robert Burton, *The Anatomy of Melancholy,* 3 vols. ed. Holborn Jackson (London: Dent, 1932), vol. 1: 144; hereafter cited in text.

4. Walter Benjamin, *Ursprung des deutschen Trauerspiels* (1928), *Gesammelte Schriften,* vol. 1 (Frankfurt: Suhrkamp, 1974), 318.

5. See Theodor W. Adorno, *Jargon der Eigentlichkeit—Zur deutschen Ideologie* (Frankfurt: Suhrkamp, 1964), 13, 66. The exemplary instance is Otto Friedrich Bollnow, *Das Wesen der Stimmungen* (Frankfurt: Klostermann, 1943), 31, 129 f.

6. See Hans Blumenberg, introduction to his *Wirklichkeiten in denen wir leben* (Stuttgart: Reclam, 1981), 6. See especially his essay "Wirklichkeitsbegriff und Möglichkeit des Romans," *Poetik und Hermeneutik,* vol. 1 (Munich: Eidos, 1964), 9–27.

7. *Ursprung des deutschen Trauerspiels,* 357. See especially his posthumous "Zentralpark," 676 (fragment 28).

8. See Northrop Frye, *Anatomy of Criticism* (Princeton: Princeton University Press, 1957), 89 ff.

9. See Michel Foucault, *Les mots et les choses* (Paris: Gallimard, 1966), 32 ff.

10. *Ursprung des deutschen Trauerspiels,* 320.

11. See G. W. Pigman, *Grief and English Renaissance Elegy* (Cambridge: Cambridge University Press, 1985).

12. See, for example, Peter M. Sacks, *The English Elegy* (Baltimore: Johns Hopkins University Press, 1985).

13. Stanley Fish, "Lycidas: A Poem Finally Anonymous," *Glyph* 8 (1981): 3, 7.

14. See Anselm Haverkamp, "Milton's Counterplot—Dekonstruction und Trauerarbeit 1637," *Deutsche Vierteljahrsschrift* 63 (1989): 608.

15. John Locke, *An Essay Concerning Human Understanding*, 2 vols., ed. Alexander Campbell Fraser (Oxford: Clarendon Press, 1959), 532.

16. See, meanwhile, Cathy Caruth, *Empirical Truths and Critical Fictions: Locke, Wordsworth, Kant, Freud* (Baltimore: Johns Hopkins University Press, 1991), 34 ff.

17. See Perry Meisel, "Freud's Reflective Realism," *October* 28 (1984): 43–59. I owe to Perry Meisel the careful reading of this chapter when it was still a paper, later to be published with his improvements in *New Literary History*.

18. Ovid, *The Fasti, Tristia, Pontic Epistles, Ibis, and Halieticon*, trans. Henry Riley (London: Bell, 1909), 247 ff.

19. See Monroe C. Beardsley, *Aesthetics: Problems in the Philosophy of Criticism* (New York: Harcourt, Brace and World, 1958), 220 ff. , 254 ff.

20. See William Empson, *Seven Types of Ambiguity* (1930), rev. ed. (New York: New Directons, 1947), 214 ff.

21. See, for example, Paul H. Fry, *The Poet's Calling in the English Ode* (New Haven: Yale University Press, 1980), 9.

22. Commentary on *Ode on Melancholy*, in her edition of *The Poems of John Keats*, 538.

23. See Aileen Ward, "Keats and Burton: A Reappraisal," *Philological Quarterly* 40 (1961): 532–52; and Robert Cummings, "Keats's Melancholy in the Temple of Delight," *Keats-Shelley Journal* 36 (1987): 50–62.

24. See Jerome J. McGann's commentary on "She Walks in Beauty," *The Complete Poetical Works of Lord Byron*, 3 vols., ed. Jerome J. McGann (Oxford: Clarendon Press, 1981), vol. 3: 467 (para. 249).

25. See Horace *Carmina* 1. 5; with the commentary by Steele Commager, *The Odes of Horace* (New Haven: Yale University Press, 1962), 67 ff.

26. *Shakespeare's Sonnets*, ed. Stephen Booth (New Haven: Yale University Press, 1977), 31.

27. Donald Barthelme, "Robert Kennedy Saved from Drowning," in his *Unspeakable Practices, Unnatural Acts* (New York: Farrar, Straus and Giroux, 1968). See his essay "Not Knowing," in *The Best American Essays 1986*, ed. Elizabeth Hardwick (New York: Ticknor and Fields, 1986), 22.

28. See Kenneth Burke, "Symbolic Action in a Poem by Keats" (1945), *A Grammar of Motives* (Berkeley: University of California Press, 1969), 447 ff.

29. See Erich Auerbach, "Figura" (1939), *Gesammelte Aufsätze zur romanischen Philologie* (Bern: Francke, 1967), 55 ff.

30. Ben Jonson, "Of Death," in *The Complete Poems*, ed. George Parfitt (New Haven: Yale University Press, 1975), 45; as quoted by Pigman, *Grief and English Renaissance Elegy*, 1.

31. Paul de Man, "Anthropomorphism and Trope in the Lyric," *The Rhetoric of Romanticism* (New York: Columbia University Press, 1984), 239 ff.

32. Earl Wasserman, *The Finer Tone: Keats' Major Poems* (Baltimore: Johns Hopkins University Press, 1953, 1967), 184.

33. See Cynthia Chase, "Viewless Wings: Keats's Ode to a Nightingale," *Decomposing Figures: Rhetorical Readings in the Romantic Tradition* (Baltimore: Johns Hopkins University Press, 1986), 70, 80.

34. Commentary on Sonnet 31, *Shakespeare's Sonnets*, 181.

35. I. A. Richards, Introduction, *Principles of Literary Criticism* (London: Routledge and Kegan Paul, 1924), vii. See Gilbert Ryle's account of that metaphor in *The Concept of Mind* (London: Hutchinson, 1949).

36. See Harold Bloom, "Keats and the Embarassments of Tradition," *From Sensibility to Romanticism*, ed. Frederick Hilles and Harold Bloom (New York: Oxford University Press, 1964), 522; see also his *Map of Misreading* (New York: Oxford University Press, 1975), 152.

37. See Joel Fineman, *Shakespeare's Perjured Eye: The Invention of Poetic Subjectivity in the Sonnets* (Berkeley: University of California Press, 1986).

38. See, for example, David Perkins, "Affirmation of Process in *Ode on Melancholy* and *To Autumn*," in *Twentieth Century Interpretations of Keats's Odes*, ed. Jack Stillinger (Englewood Cliffs: Prentice Hall, 1968), 85–93.

Bibliography

This bibliography includes only works relevant to the arguments elaborated in this book. Further references are to be found in the footnotes. With few exceptions, no attempt has been made to add the more recent literature. Quotations from the German texts of Hölderlin's works are taken from Friedrich Beissner's Stuttgart Edition—the poems *Andenken* and *Mnemosyne* from vol. 2 ("Dichtungen nach 1800"). The poems *Das fröhliche Leben* and *Der Kirchhof* are taken from vol. 9 ("Dichtungen nach 1806, Mündliches") of Dietrich E. Sattler's Frankfurt Edition. Albrecht von Haller's *Unvollendete Ode* is quoted according to the text established by Karl S. Guthke in *Deutsche Vierteljahrsschrift für Literaturwissenschaft und Geistesgeschichte* 48 (1974), 542–545; *Doris*, the *Trauerode*, and other poems on Mariane are taken from the edition of Haller's works by Adolf Frey in the series *Deutsche National Literatur*, vols. 41–42 (1893). All poems have been newly translated by Vernon Chadwick for the purposes of this book, departing from the existing Hölderlin translations by Michael Hamburger (1964) and Richard Sieburth (1984).

Abraham, Nicholas and Maria Torok. *Cryptonymie—Le verbier de l'Homme aux loups.* Paris: Aubier-Flammarion, 1975.

———. *L'écorce et le noyau.* Paris: Aubier-Flammarion, 1978.

Adorno, Theodor W. *Gesammelte Schriften.* 20 vols. to date. Frankfurt: Suhrkamp, 1970– .

Beissner, Friedrich. *Hölderlin–Reden und Aufsätze.* 1961. Köln-Wien: Böhlau, 1969.

Benjamin, Walter. *Gesammelte Schriften.* 7 vols. to date. Frankfurt: Suhrkamp, 1972– .

Bertaux, Pierre. *Friedrich Hölderlin.* Frankfurt: Suhrkamp, 1978.

———. *Hölderlin-Variationen.* Frankfurt: Suhrkamp, 1984.

Binder, Wolfgang. *Hölderlin-Aufsätze.* Frankfurt: Insel, 1970.

———. "Hölderlin: 'Andenken.'" *Turm-Vorträge 1985–86.* Ed. Uvo Hölscher. Tübingen: Hölderlin-Gesellschaft, 1986. 5–30.

Bloom, Harold. *The Anxiety of Influence.* New York: Oxford University Press, 1973.

———. *A Map of Misreading.* New York: Oxford University Press, 1975.

Blumenberg, Hans. *Arbeit am Mythos.* Frankfurt: Suhrkamp, 1979.

———. *Lebenszeit und Weltzeit.* Frankfurt: Suhrkamp, 1986.

———. *Paradigmen zu einer Metaphorologie.* Bonn: Bouvier, 1960.

Böschenstein, Bernhard. *Hölderlins Rheinhymne.* 1959. Zürich: Atlantis, 1968.

———. *Konkordanz zu Hölderlins Gedichten nach 1800.* Göttingen: Vandenhoek & Ruprecht, 1964.

———. "Hölderlins späteste Gedichte." *Hölderlin-Jahrbuch* 14 (1965–66). 35–56.

———. *Frucht des Gewitters: Hölderlins Dionysos als Gott der Revolution.* Frankfurt: Insel, 1989.

Böschenstein-Schäfer, Renate. "Die Stimme der Muse in Hölderlins Gedichten." *Hölderlin-Jahrbuch* 24 (1984–85). 87–112.

———. "Hölderlins allegorische Ausdrucksform, untersucht an der Hymne 'An die Madonna.'" *Jenseits des Idealismus: Hölderlins letzte Homburger Jahre (1804–1806)*. Ed. Christoph Jamme and Otto Pöggeler. Bonn: Bouvier, 1988. 181–209.

Bröcker, Walter. *Das was kommt, gesehen von Nietzsche und Hölderlin*. Pfullingen: Neske, 1963.

Bröcker-Oltmanns, Käte. "Die Schuld des Dichters (zu Hölderlins Hymne 'Der Einzige')." *Lexis* II (1949), fasc. 1. 155–160.

Chase, Cynthia. *Decomposing Figures: Rhetorical Readings in the Romantic Tradition*. Baltimore: Johns Hopkins University Press, 1986.

———. "Primary Narcissism and the Giving of Figure." *Abjection, Melancholia, and Love*. Ed. John Fletcher and Andrew Benjamin. London: Blackwell, 1990. 124–136.

Cool, Kenneth. "The Petrarchan Landscape as Palimpsest." *Journal of Medieval and Renaissance Studies* 11 (1981). 83–100.

Courcelle, Pierre. *Recherches sur les Confessions de Saint Augustin*. 1950. Paris, 1968.

De Man, Paul. *Blindness and Insight: Essays in the Rhetoric of Contemporary Criticism*. 1972. Minneapolis: Minnesota University Press, 1983.

———. *Allegories of Reading*. New Haven: Yale University Press, 1979.

———. *The Rhetoric of Romanticism*. New York: Columbia University Press, 1984.

———. *Critical Writings 1953–1978*. Minneapolis: Minnesota University Press, 1988.

Derrida, Jacques. *La carte postale de Socrate à Freud et au-delà*. Paris: Galilée, 1980.

———. *L'Écriture et la différence*. Paris: Minuit, 1967.

———. *Marges de la philosophie*. Paris: Minuit, 1972.

———. *Memoires for Paul de Man*. New York: Columbia University Press, 1986.

———. Preface ("FORS"). *Cryptonymie—Le verbier de l'Homme aux loups*. By Nicholas Abraham and Maria Torok. Paris: Aubier-Flammarion, 1975.

———. *Psyché—Inventions de l'autre*. Paris: Galilée, 1987.

———. "The Politics of Friendship." *Journal of Philosophy* 85 (1988). 632–644.

Dilthey, Wilhelm. *Das Erlebnis und die Dichtung*. Leipzig: Teubner, 1906.

Empson, William. *Seven Types of Ambiguity*. 1930. New York: New Directions, 1947.

Felman, Shoshana. "Turning the Screw of Interpretation." *Yale French Studies* 55–56 (1977). 94–207.

Foucault, Michel. "Le *non* du père." *Critique* 178 (1962). 195–209.

Franz, Michael. "Annäherung an Hölderlins Verrücktheit." *Hölderlin-Jahrbuch* 22 (1981–82). 274–294.

Freccero, John. "The Figtree and the Laurel: Petrarch's Poetics." *Literary Theory/Renaissance Texts*. Ed. Patricia Parker and David Quint. Baltimore: Johns Hopkins University Press, 1986. 20–32.

———. *Dante: The Poetics of Conversion*. Cambridge: Harvard University Press, 1986.

Freud, Sigmund. *Studienausgabe*. 12 vols. to date. Frankfurt: Fischer, 1969– .

Fried, Michael. *Absorption and Theatricality: Painting and Beholder in the Age of Diderot*. Chicago: Chicago University Press, 1980.

Fry, Paul. "Non-Constitution: History, Structure, and the Occasion of the Literary." *Yale Journal of Criticism* 1:2 (1987–88). 45–64.

Greisch, Jean. "Les mots et les roses: La métaphore chez Martin Heidegger." *Revue des sciences philosophique et théologiques* 57 (1973). 443–456.

———. "Faire entendre l'Origine en son pur surgissement (Hölderlin et Heidegger)." *Hölderlin vu de France*. Ed. Bernhard Böschenstein and Jacques le Rider. Tübingen: Narr, 1987. 113–128.

Guthke, Karl S. "Hallers 'Unvollkommene Ode über die Ewigkeit': Veranlassung und Entstehung." *Deutsche Vierteljahrsschrift* 48 (1974). 528–545.

Hamlin, Cyrus. "Die Poetik des Gedächtnisses." *Hölderlin-Jahrbuch* 24 (1984–85). 119–138.

————. *The Task of Interpretation: The Hermeneutics of Hölderlin's "Patmos."* Unpublished ms., 1987.

Harrison, Robin B. *Hölderlin and Greek Literature.* Oxford: Oxford University Press, 1975.

————. "Das Rettende oder Gefahr? Die Bedeutung des Gedächtnisses in Hölderlins Hymne 'Mnemosyne.'" *Hölderlin-Jahrbuch* 24 (1984–85). 195–206.

Hartman, Geoffrey. *The Fate of Reading.* Chicago: Chicago University Press, 1975.

————. *Criticism in the Wilderness.* New Haven: Yale University Press, 1980.

————. *Saving the Text: Literature/Derrida/Philosophy.* Baltimore: Johns Hopkins University Press, 1981.

Haverkamp, Anselm. "Saving the Subject: Randbemerkungen zur Veränderung der Lyrik." *Poetica* 14 (1982). 70–91.

————. "Milton's Counterplot—Dekonstruktion und Trauerarbeit 1637: 'Lycidas.'" *Deutsche Vierteljahrsschrift* 63 (1989). 608–627.

————. "Fest/Schrift: Festschreibung unbeschreiblicher Feste in Klopstocks 'Ode von der Fahrt auf der Zürchersee.'" *Poetik und Hermeneutik.* Vol. 14 (1989). 276–298.

————. "Auswendigkeit: Das Gedächtnis der Rhetorik." *Gedächtniskunst: Raum-Schrift-Bild.* Ed. Anselm Haverkamp and Renate Lachmann. Frankfurt: Suhrkamp, 1991. 25–52.

————. "Rhetoric, Law, and the Poetics of Memory." *Cardozo Law Review* 13 (1992). 1639–1653.

————. "Notes on the Dialectical Image (How Deconstructive is It?)." *Diacritics* 22:3–4 (1992). 70–81.

————. "A Kaleidoscope of Mourning." *Pequod* 35 (1993). 13–23.

Heidegger, Martin. *Hölderlin und das Wesen der Dichtung.* Munich: Langen/Müller, 1937.

———. *Erläuterungen zu Hölderlins Dichtung.* 1951. Vol. 4 of *Gesamtausgabe.* Ed. Friedrich-Wilhelm von Herrmann. Frankfurt: Klostermann, 1982. 33–48.

———. *Unterwegs zur Sprache.* Pfullingen: Neske, 1959.

———. *Hölderlins Hymne "Andenken."* 1941–42. Vol. 52 of *Gesamtausgabe.* Ed. Curd Ochwadt. Frankfurt: Klostermann, 1982.

Hellingrath, Norbert von. *Pindarübertragungen von Hölderlin— Prolegomena zu einer Erstausgabe.* Jena, 1911.

———. *Hölderlin—Zwei Vorträge.* München: Bruckmann, 1921.

———. *Hölderlin-Vermächtnis.* 1936. Ed. Ludwig von Pigenot. München, 1944.

Henrich, Dieter. *Hegel im Kontext.* Frankfurt: Suhrkamp, 1971.

———. *Der Gang des Andenkens: Beobachtungen und Gedanken zu Hölderlins Gedicht.* Stuttgart: Klett-Cotta, 1986.

———. *Der Grund im Bewußtsein: Untersuchungen zu Hölderlins Denken (1794–1795).* Stuttgart: Klett-Cotta, 1992.

Hof, Walter. "'Mnemosyne' und die Interpretation der letzten hymnischen Versuche Hölderlins," *Germanisch-romanische Monatsschrift* 32 (1982). 418–430.

Homann, Renate. "Das Besondere und das Allgemeine in der Dichtung." *Zeitschrift für philosophische Forschung* 42 (1988). 620–644.

Ischer, Anna. *Albrecht von Haller und das klassische Altertum.* Bern, 1928.

Iser, Wolfgang. "Figurationen des lyrischen Subjekts." *Poetik und Hermeneutik.* Vol. 8. (1979). 746–749.

Jacobs, Carol. *Dissimulating Harmony: The Image of Interpretation.* Baltimore: Johns Hopkins University Press, 1978.

Jakobson, Roman. *Hölderlin, Klee, Brecht: Zur Wortkunst dreier Gedichte.* Frankfurt: Suhrkamp, 1975.

————. *Poetik—Ausgewählte Aufsätze 1921–71*. Frankfurt: Suhrkamp, 1979.

Jonas, Hans. "The Nobility of Sight." *Philosophy and Phenomenological Research* 14 (1953–54). 507–519.

Kalász, Claudia. *Hölderlin: Die poetische Kritik instrumenteller Rationalität*. München, 1988.

Kerényi, Karl. "Hölderlins Vollendung." *Hölderlin-Jahrbuch* 8 (1954). 25–45.

Kommerell, Max. *Der Dichter als Führer in der deutschen Klassik*. 1929. Frankfurt: Klostermann, 1948.

————. *Gedanken über Gedichte*. 1944. Frankfurt: Klostermann, 1956.

Krautter, Konrad. *Die Renaissance der Bukolik in der lateinischen Literatur des XIV. Jahrhunderts: von Dante bis Petrarca*. München: Fink, 1983.

Küchenhoff, Joachim, and Peter Warsitz. "Die Spur des ganz Anderen: Freuds Nosographie und der psychotische Text am Beispiel Hölderlin." *Fragmente* 17–18 (1985). 205–231.

Kudszus, Winfried. *Sprachverlust und Sinnwandel: Zur späten und spätesten Lyrik Hölderlins*. Stuttgart: Metzler, 1969.

Lacan, Jacques. *Écrits*. Paris: Seuil, 1966.

————. *Télévision*. Paris: Seuil, 1974.

————. *Les quatre concepts fondamentaux de la psychanalyse—Le séminaire XI, 1964*. Paris: Seuil, 1973.

————. *Des Psychoses—Le séminaire III, 1955–56*. Paris: Seuil, 1981.

Lacoue-Labarthe, Philippe. "The Caesura of the Speculative." *Glyph* 4 (1978). 57–84.

————. *Le sujet de la philosophie*. Paris: Aubier-Flammarion, 1979.

————. *Typographies*. Ed. Christopher Fynsk. Cambridge: Harvard University Press, 1993.

Laplanche, Jean. *Hölderlin et la question du père*. Paris: PUF, 1961.

————. *Vie et mort en psychanalyse*. Paris: Flammarion, 1970.

Lefebvre, Jean Pierre. "Auch die Stege sind Holzwege." *Hölderlin vu de France*. Ed. Bernhard Böschenstein and Jacques le Rider. Tübingen: Narr, 1987. 53–76.

Levinas, Emanuel. *Die Spur des Anderen*. Freiburg: Alber, 1983.

Liebrucks, Bruno. *"Und"—Die Sprache Hölderlins in der Spannweite von Mythos und Logos, Realität und Wirklichkeit*. Frankfurt, 1979.

Lipps, Hans. *Untersuchungen zu einer hermeneutischen Logik*. 1938. Frankfurt: Klostermann, 1968.

Lobsien, Eckhard. *Landschaft in Texten*. Stuttgart: Metzler, 1981.

Lypp, Bernhard. *Ästhetischer Absolutismus und politische Vernunft*. Frankfurt: Suhrkamp, 1972.

———. "'Mein ist die Rede vom Vaterland': Heidegger und Hölderlin." *Merkur* 41:456 (1987). 120–135.

———. "Hölderlins 'Mnemosyne.'" *Das Rätsel der Zeit*. Ed. Hans Michael Baumgartner. Freiburg: Alber, 1993. 291–330.

Marquard, Odo. *Skeptische Methode im Blick auf Kant*. Freiburg: Alber, 1958.

———. *Abschied vom Prinzipiellen*. Stuttgart: Reclam, 1981.

Menke, Bettine. *Sprachfiguren: Name-Allegorie-Bild nach Walter Benjamin*. (Diss. Konstanz, 1986). München: Fink, 1991.

Meyer-Kalkus, Reinhard. "Mnemosyne." *Historisches Wörterbuch der Philosophie*. Vol. 5. Basel: Schwabe 1974. 1442.

Miller, J. Hillis. *The Ethics of Reading*. New York: Columbia Univeristy Press, 1987.

Nägele, Rainer. "Friedrich Hölderlin: Die F(V)erse des Achilles." *Fragment und Totalität*. Ed. Lucien Dällenbach and Christiaan L. Hart Nibbrig. Frankfurt: Suhrkamp, 1984. 200–211.

———. *Text, Geschichte und Subjektivität in Hölderlins Dichtung: "Uneßbarer Schrift gleich."* Stuttgart: Metzler, 1985.

Nagy, Gregory. *The Best of the Achaeans*. Baltimore: Johns Hopkins University Press, 1979.

Nancy, Jean-Luc. *Logodaedalus—Le discours de la syncope*. Vol. 1. Paris: Aubier-Flammarion, 1976.

Philipsen, Bart. "De *arme* Hölderlin en de politiek van de dwaasheid." *Pi—Tijdschrift voor Poezie* 6:4 (1987). 46–59.

———. "'Mit Untertänigkeit Scardanelli'—Toenadering tot de 'Idylle' van Hölderlins laatste Gedichten." *Restant* 15:2 (1987). 195–219.

———. "'En lees mij, o gij bloesems van Duitsland"—Hölderlins late Hymnen." *In het licht van de letter: Zes oefeningen in deconstructie.* Ed. Herman Servotte, Ludo Verbeeck, and Dirk de Schutter. Leuven: Peeters, 1988. 57–81.

———. "Herz aus Glas: Hölderlin, Rousseau und das blöde Subjekt der Moderne." *Bild-Sprache* [Festschrift Ludo Verbeeck]. Leuven: Universitaire Pers, 1990. 177–194.

———. *Die List der Einfalt: Eine Nachlese zu Hölderlins spätester Dichtung.* (Diss. KU Leuven, 1992). Munich: Fink, 1995.

Pigman, G. W. *Grief and English Renaissance Elegy.* Cambridge: Cambridge University Press, 1985.

Reinhardt, Karl. *Vermächtnis der Antike.* Göttingen: Vandenhoek und Ruprecht, 1960.

Ricoeur, Paul. *Le conflit des interprétations.* Paris: Seuil, 1970.

———. *La métaphore vive.* Paris: Seuil, 1975.

Roland-Jensen, Flemming. "Hölderlins Mnemosyne." *Zeitschrift für deutsche Philologie* 98 (1979). 201–241.

———. *Hölderlins Muse: Edition und Interpretation der Hymne "Die Nymphe Mnemosyne."* Würzburg: Könighausen und Neumann, 1989.

Ronell, Avital. *Dictations: On Haunted Writing.* Bloomington: Indiana University Press, 1986.

Ryan, Lawrence J. *Hölderlins Lehre vom Wechsel der Töne.* Stuttgart: Kohlhamer, 1960.

Sattler, D. E. *Friedrich Hölderlin—144 fliegende Briefe.* 2 vols. Darmstadt-Neuwied: Luchterhand, 1981.

———. "'al rovescio'"—Hölderlin nach 1806." *Le pauvre Holterling* 7 (1984). 17–28.

Schmidt, Jochen. "Der Begriff des Zorns in Hölderlins Spätwerk." *Hölderlin-Jahrbuch* 15 (1967–68). 128–157.

————. *Hölderlins letzte Hymnen: Andenken und Mnemosyne.* Tübingen: Mohr, 1970.

————. "Sobria ebrietatis: Hölderlins 'Hälfte des Lebens.'" *Hölderlin-Jahrbuch* 23 (1982–83). 182–190.

Schöne, Albrecht. *Emblematik und Drama im Zeitalter des Barock.* München: Beck, 1964.

Schutter, Dirk de. "Words like Stones." *(Dis-)continuities: Essays on Paul de Man.* Ed. Luc Herman, Kris Humbeeck, and Geert Lernout. Amsterdam, 1990. 99–110.

Starobinski, Jean. "Ironie et Mélancholie: Gozzi, Hoffmann, Kierkegaard." *Critique* 227–228 (1966). 291–308, 438–457.

————. *Trois fureurs.* Paris: Gallimard, 1975.

————. "Le rire de Démocrite (Mélancolie et réflexion)." *Bulletin de la Sociéte francaise de Philosophie* 83:1 (1989).

————. *La mélancolie au miroir—Trois lectures de Baudelaire.* Paris: Julliard, 1989.

Stäuble, Eduard. "Albrecht von Haller, der Dichter zwischen den Zeiten." *Der Deutschunterricht* 8 (1956). 5–29.

————. *Albrecht von Haller "Über den Ursprung des Übels."* Zürich: Atlantis, 1959.

Stierle, Karlheinz. "Die Identität des Gedichts—Hölderlin als Paradigma." *Poetik und Hermeneutik.* Vol. 8. (1979). 505–552.

Stierlin, Helm. *Das Tun des Einen ist das Tun des Anderen.* Frankfurt: Suhrkamp, 1971.

————. "Creativity and Schizophrenic Psychosis as Reflected in Hölderlins Fate." *Hölderlin—An Early Modern,* ed. Emory E. George. Ann Arbor: University of Michigan Press, 1972. 215.

Szondi, Peter. *Hölderlin-Studien.* Frankfurt: Insel, 1967.

————. *Einführung in die literarische Hermeneutik.* Frankfurt: Suhrkamp, 1975.

Verbeeck, Ludo. "Récit mythique ou appel transgressiv? A propos du poème 'Der Winkel von Hardt' de Friedrich Hölderlin." *Mélanges de linguistique et de littérature* [Festschrift Henri Draye]. Louvain: Nauwelaerts, 1978. 231–239.

Vietor, Karl. *Geschichte der deutschen Ode.* München: Drei Masken, 1923.

Warminski, Andrzej. *Readings in Interpretation: Hölderlin, Hegel, Heidegger.* Minneapolis: Minnesota University Press, 1987.

Weber, Samuel. *Freud-Legende.* Olten: Walter, 1978.

———. *Institution and Interpretation.* Minneapolis: Minnesota University Press, 1986.

Winkler, Eugen Gottlob. *Eugen Gottlob Winkler.* Selected and edited by Walter Jens. Frankfurt: Fischer, 1960.

Zuberbühler, Rolf. *Hölderlins Erneuerung der Sprache aus ihren etymologischen Ursprüngen.* Berlin: Erich Schmidt, 1960.

BIBLIOGRAPHY

Subject Index

Name Index